Journal of a Voyage up the Mediterranean
by Charles Swan

Address:
HardPress
8345 NW 66TH ST #2561
MIAMI FL 33166-2626
USA
Email: info@hardpress.net

JOURNAL

OF A

VOYAGE UP THE MEDITERRANEAN;

PRINCIPALLY AMONG THE

ISLANDS OF THE ARCHIPELAGO,

AND IN

ASIA MINOR:

INCLUDING MANY INTERESTING PARTICULARS RELATIVE TO

The Greek Revolution,

ESPECIALLY A JOURNEY THROUGH MAINA TO THE CAMP OF IBRAHIM PACHA,

TOGETHER WITH OBSERVATIONS ON

THE ANTIQUITIES, OPINIONS, AND USAGES OF GREECE, AS THEY NOW EXIST.

TO WHICH IS ADDED,

AN ESSAY ON THE FANARIOTES,

translated from the French of

MARK PHILIP ZALLONY, A GREEK.

By the REV. CHARLES SWAN,

LATE OF CATHARINE HALL, CAMBRIDGE ; CHAPLAIN TO H. M. S. CAMBRIAN ;
AUTHOR OF SERMONS ON SEVERAL SUBJECTS, AND TRANSLATOR OF THE GESTA ROMANORUM.

" Whilk were fools, and whilk were wise,
And whilk of them could most quaintyse ;
And whilk did wrong, and whilk right,
And whilk maintained peace and fight—
Of their deeds shall be my sawe,
In what time, and of what law."
Chronicle of Robert de Brunne.

IN TWO VOLUMES.

VOL. I.

LONDON:

PRINTED FOR C. AND J. RIVINGTON,
ST. PAUL'S CHURCH-YARD,
WATERLOO-PLACE, AND 148, STRAND

1826.

LONDON :
PRINTED BY R. GILBERT,
ST. JOHN'S SQUARE.

ADVERTISEMENT.

MESSRS. RIVINGTON respectfully inform the public, that the Work now submitted to their inspection, is printed from the Manuscripts transmitted to them by the author for that purpose.

They trust, that on examination, it will be found to contain a variety of entertaining matter respecting the Greeks, as well as much information which must be peculiarly interesting at the present period.

The indulgence of the reader is requested for any trifling inaccuracies; as on account of the author's absence from the country, it was not possible for him to superintend the progress of his work through the press.

WATERLOO-PLACE,
May 3, 1826.

CONTENTS.

VOL. I.

CHAPTER I.

CHAPTER II.

CHAPTER III.

CHAPTER IV.

CHAPTER V.

CHAPTER VI.

VOL. II.

CHAPTER XI.

CHAPTER XII.

15

CHAPTER XIII.

CHAPTER XIV.

CHAPTER XV.

CHAPTER XVI.

CHAPTER XVII.

ESSAY ON THE FANARIOTES.

CHAPTER I.

CHAPTER II.

CHAPTER III.

CHAPTER IV.

CHAPTER V.

CONCLUSIONS

DRAWN FROM THE PRECEDING CHAPTERS.

ERRATA.

VOL. I.

Page 174, line 4 from bottom, *for* Peleon *read* Pelion
——— 188, — 4 from bottom, *for* son *read* son-in-law
——— 189, — 5, *for* father *read* father-in-law
——— 244, — 3 from bottom, for *manekin* read *manikin*
——— 337, — last, for *conscentia* read *conscientia*

VOL. II.

Page 70, line 2 from bottom, *for* omenous *read* ominous
——— 75, — 12, *for* dumfounded *read* dumbfounded
——— 80, — 11, *for* I forgot *read* I have forgot
——— 115, — 12, *for* Bobalina *read* Bobolino
——— 131, — 5 from bottom, for *Fanarcotes* read *Fanariotes*
——— 161, — 6, *for* Vironne et Leiback *read* Verone et Laybach
——— 175, — 6, *for* Guenara *read* Guevara

A

JOURNAL,

&c. &c.

CHAPTER I.

WE lost sight of England on the 12th of October, 1824. Captain Fox, a son of Lord Holland, with his lady, a daughter of his Royal Highness the Duke of Clarence; Mr. Tennant, a relative of my Lord Yarborough; his medical attendant; and a Mr. Hall, were cabin passengers: a son of General Slade also partook of the gun-room mess.

Sunday, 17*th Oct.*——This morning the service of the church was performed on the main deck. I observed, with pleasure, the attention of the seamen; who were, for the most part, regular in making the responses. About three o'clock P.M. we came in sight of the coast of Portugal; the royal palace of Mafra was distinctly perceptible, together with the town of Cintra. White houses glittering in the sun, united with the convent-crested granite rock, formed a sweetly picturesque object from the ship.

Monday, 18*th Oct.*——Passed Cape St. Vincent and Sagras about ten o'clock this morning; the ship running before the wind. In Moore's words:

> " The sea was like an azure lake,
>   And o'er its calm the vessel glides
>   Gently, as if it fear'd to wake
>   The anger of the slumb'ring tides."

Towards evening the wind totally subsided; and a sky radiant as the imagination could picture, gratified the sight. A broad golden line was thrown by the setting sun upon the waters; while the small barks (some of which were distinguished by the triangular *felucca* sail) moved slowly and gracefully along. On the Spanish coast Cape St. Maria presented itself with the mountains of Moncheque, enveloped in a soft blue mist. The porpoise gamboled around the ship, as the sailors did within it. The fiddle put the limbs of the crew in motion, while the band on the quarter deck was employed in facilitating the officers' execution of quadrilles. Mrs. Fox joined in them with much spirit.

Tuesday, 19th Oct.—The wind becoming contrary during the night, we were driven back to the South coast of Portugal, and came within a few miles of Faro, a city of some magnitude. We observed the cathedral very distinctly.

Friday, 22d Oct.—The continuation of adverse winds induced the captain to put into Cadiz. At some distance from the town we took up a Spaniard. He had a singularly intelligent countenance; and his round hat of grey cloth, blue naval jacket, and scarlet sash tied tightly to the waist, presented an object which pleased perhaps from its novelty. A signal gun being fired for a pilot, a boat put off from the shore, and brought out a little fat man, whose appearance indicated a deep feeling of self-importance, which was rendered truly ridiculous by his diminutive height and *oleaginousness* *. Cadiz has an imposing as-

* In a country of *olives* and *olive-yards*, perhaps such a word may be admissible. The term is not a bad one; and describes well enough the *oily sudatory* character of the Spanish countenance not uncommon amongst the lower orders.

pect from the sea. Its regularly built houses
of white stone shine gaily in the sun; and in
addition to this, the numerous fleet of ships
stationed off the town—some with their sails
set, others at anchor, interspersed with a variety of *feluccas*, cruising up and down on the
beautiful morning of our arrival, were extremely enlivening. The fat pilot, on being
desired to allow as much time as possible for
the crew to take their *wine*, (such is the liberal
establishment of the British navy!) with much
of his country's haughtiness, replied, " that
they would have time enough to take it afterwards," colouring at the same moment to the
very brow, even through the dinginess of his
sun-burnt complexion. It seemed to me a
characteristic introduction to the land and the
people—to that people who formerly required
the Persian monarch, when addressing their
king, to superscribe his epistles,—" AU ROI
QUI A LE SOLEIL POUR CHAPEAU *." Several French men of war are stationed off
Cadiz; and a French garrison, we are told, is
quartered in the town.

* See Moreri.

Saturday, 23d Oct.—I arose this morning at an early hour, that I might the more speedily gratify my curiosity in Cadiz. The approach to this place from the water is fine, and of a kind altogether new. The uniform and white-washed fronts of the houses, surmounted generally by a small turret, have a particularly pleasing effect, and render Cadiz a great attraction to foreigners. The first thing that struck me after passing the batteries, was the market. The peculiar cries of the venders of fruit and poultry, with their not less peculiar appearance, operated powerfully upon my risible faculties. Wandering along at random, I accidentally turned into the old magnificent cathedral of Cadiz; which is, and, I understand, has long been, in a state of repair. A great length of time must elapse before its completion, which, indeed, may never take place: for the distresses brought upon the town by the revolution, have exhausted the funds of the ecclesiastics, not less than the property of the citizens. As much as they have done, however, to this building, is singularly beautiful. It displays much classical taste; and its execution equals the design.

From hence I turned to the convent of the Augustines. A number of females were offering up their orisons—such at least *ought* to have been their employment. But though their " lips moved, there was war in the heart." One damsel knelt before a small crucifix—her arms folded, so as to bring the fan which was contained in her right hand into pretty good play. This genial weapon, the auxiliary of love or war, was kept in constant motion ; while her eyes, rambling about as much as the position of the body would admit, were attracted to every object, save that which it might have been presumed she was contemplating. Another, almost illimitable in bulk, with the utmost difficulty, " screwed" herself up to a " sticking-place." She reached, with laudable exertion, the very steps of the altar, and there, as overcome by the unusual effort, squatted motionless on the ground. This is a common posture, and seems, among innumerable others, the remains of Moorish habits.

Like all the buildings of Roman Catholic worship, the one in question (which is the chapel of the Augustine monastery) is adorned with a bewildering profusion of gold and silver—

" wax, stone, wood," &c. : and unquestionably
is " wondrous fine." But the impression left
upon my mind was, that their devotion had
converted the temple of the Deity into a toy-
shop—the women into arrant coquettes, not to
say worse; and the men into bigots. The
mummery, so universally practised here, was
disgusting enough; and seems to me the very
last stage of a confirmed idiotcy. In consecrating the host, we remark that the priest first
bows to the crucifix, then elevates the cup as if
to examine whether the expected liquid begins
to flow, and how far it has risen. By and bye
his hand is extended toward the crucifix, and
wafted backwards and forwards from the cross
to the cup, with the intent, as well as one can
judge, of transferring the holiness of the relic
to the wine he is about to administer. To this
succeed bows and bell-ringing, touching of
noses and chins and breasts, which last is understood to typify the cross. Representations
of saints, angels, virgins, and cherubs in every
state and stage of beauty and deformity may
here be met with ; the most unhappy " pagod-
looking things" by the side of the ecstatic,
downcast, dreary countenance of the blessed

10

virgin, or beatified saint. One of the latter
I noticed elevating his head a considerable
distance above his shoulders; and another,
who was transfixed with nearly a dozen arrows;
judging by the placid expression of the mar-
tyr's face, this might have been the pleasantest
thing in the world. A multitude of weeping
Magdalenes, bedizened in the finest apparel,
meet the eye at every turn; and their sorrow-
touched aspects, besmeared with a sufficiency
of oil, give them a most sudatory character;
and this, I apprehend, is intended : the agony
of their souls is presumed to facilitate a copious
sweat, and to typify the exudation of mortal
sin ! It is remarkable, that while they enjoin
the votaries of religion in this world, to discard
the vanities of dress, they heap together upon
these exemplars of sanctity, these waxen per-
sonifications of good manners, all the gewgaws
that female fancy could devise, or the female
heart covet. Surely the prayer that is offered
up at shrines so decorated, must needs parti-
cipate in this their most palpable characteristic; and instead of suggesting to the mind
devout sentiments, are more calculated to call
up from the innermost recesses of the heart the

dormant feelings of worldly vanity. The head-
gear of Jezebel will fix the attention under
these circumstances sooner than the Song of
Deborah.

> " RELIGION, erst so venerable,
> What art thou now, but made a fable?
> A holy mask on Folly's brow;
> Where under lies Dissimulation,
> Lined with all abomination,—
> Sacred Religion! where art thou * ?"

At a Café where the waiters spoke but little
French I had some difficulty in making myself
understood: after many trials, one of them
brought pen and ink, and with much delibera-
tion and affected solemnity scrawled " *Non
intelligo tuam linguam.*" Here was at least a
guide for future communication: and though
the latinity of this erudite " slave of the coffee-
cup" was, as might have been expected, of the
worst description, it was more intelligible than
his French. I was curious to know where he
had acquired his learning, and to what end he
had dedicated any portion of time to that

* Joshua Sylvester.

which he must have found a very useless attainment. With the precision of a parrot,
however, his only answer was " *Ego sum sco-
lasticus*" or " *Ego Josephus à Lestone*," &c.
&c. Josephus seemed very proud of his knowledge, and not less of the opportunity (which
I fancy occurred but seldom) of displaying it.
In proof thereof he honoured me with a very
cordial shake of the hand at parting. I did
not see him again, but in a subsequent part of
the day, having occasion to pass the door of
his Café, I distinctly heard a sonorous " Monsieur, Monsieur !" which it did not at that
time altogether suit me to reply to.

The rest of this day was consumed in stroll-
ing about the streets of Cadiz. The loftiness
of the houses, not less than their regularity,
has a pleasing appearance. The windows are
generally covered with an iron grating, in most
cases painted green, which forms a good contrast to the whiteness of the walls. The extreme vicinity of the opposite side of the street
makes these gratings necessary for the inhabitants; and if the female part of them is as
much addicted to intrigue as report avers, it
is well that even *such* precaution is adopted.

There is most commonly a balcony to every window. The lower parts of these dwellings are used as warehouses, and sometimes as stables, to which you enter by an immense door, full of iron knobs. The richer sort have them of brass, which they keep in a high state of polish. On passing through this door the visitor is brought into a small square area, which is the centre of the mansion, and being uncovered, serves to admit the air to every part of the building: around the square are the apartments of the family. In some instances the area contains a fountain, which, of course, contributes much to the coolness of the place. To the great door is attached a string, which is carried into the apartment above: when any one knocks, the door immediately opens, and you enter without observing by whom you are admitted, or to whom you are to address yourself. But a voice presently directs your ascent, and you then enter the room inhabited by the family without troubling its inmates to descend and receive your message.

The women appear but little restricted in their actions; and the crowds that flock to the

Alameyda, a fashionable promenade, which almost every town in Spain is provided with, gives occasion to a world of coquetry, and, as I fear, to all its concomitant evils. The inhabitants begin to assemble about five o'clock, the females possessing themselves of stone seats arranged on each side of the Alameyda; here they sit for the inspection of those who please to honour them with their notice. I have seen servant girls in England drawn up in ranks to be hired, and I have observed cattle penned up in Smithfield for sale; the obliging reader may adopt whichever similitude he considers good—he will not err greatly in either.

Of the beauty of Spanish women, much has been said; but the specimens which are to be found in Cadiz do not justify the character, at least so far as they fell under my observation. They have almost universally brilliant eyes; but, some few excepted, their features are without regularity, and possess a degree of harshness, which, I need scarcely add, age does not improve: the majority of them are corpulent and gross; and though the eye loses little of its lustre by time, yet the face acquires an early coarseness, and a sallower tinge. The precocity of the Spaniards is one cause of this, but more probably it is to be attributed to matrimony contracted in extreme youth. " The hasty marriages in tender years," said the discerning Raleigh, " wherein nature being but yet green and growing, we rent from her, and replant her branches, while herself hath not yet any root sufficient to maintain her own top ; and such half-ripe seeds (for the most part) in the growing up wither in the bud, and wax old even in their infancy *." Such is the case precisely with the women in Spain ; a very few years destroys whatever beauty they could once boast, and leaves them not only destitute of every personal grace, but utterly repulsive and disgusting. What effect this rapid degeneracy of the body has upon the mind, is a question I can only guess at. Bigotry and an increased splenetic temperament are not unlikely sometimes to result—a rigid unconciliating feeling—happy in being the cause of unhappiness to others, and in cherishing, to the close of life, a rankling jealousy, which,

---

* Hist. of the World, Book I. p. 46. fol.

in the regret it treasures for departed graces,
would blast every bud as it expands itself in
early beauty, and spread around the contami-
nation of a diseased mind and a wasting body.

The dress of Spanish females is similar in
all the grades of society, with the exception, of
course, that finer materials are used by the
more wealthy. Their walking habiliment consists of a black gown, covering the neck ; the
hinder part of the head is enveloped in a black
lace mantle, or in a black silk one with a broad
border of lace. This costume to the elder
part of society is very unfavourable. It exhibits a few dirty grey hairs straggling over a
sallow wrinkled forehead, the delicacy of the
Spanish women seldom inducing them to
cleanse the hair of the scurf to which it is
more than commonly liable.

This evening we witnessed the performance
of a new Spanish play. The author was neither
more nor less than the Señor who represented
one of the principal characters. Our party,
not understanding the language, thought it
intolerably dull ; there was no incident, and
so few characters as to make much incident
nearly impossible. The speeches were inordi-

mately long; and an occasional laugh, whether
at the play, or at the man, or at both, was the
only indication of public applause. They remained, however, to the conclusion, with a
most assiduous and laudable patience, and
then rewarded the actor-author with a few re-
freshing plaudits. Surely, thought I, 'tis a
good-natured people! The language seems
sonorous, though without the musical cadence
of the Italian.

Sunday, 24th Oct. — The soldiers of the
French garrison attended mass at the Church
of San Francisco; they entered in full military
array, under arms: the officers only were uncovered during the service.

The Alameyda was, this evening, crowded
to excess; and exhibited, in a few instances,
gayer colours than ordinary. For some reason
or other, there was no opera—a good precedent, but of great singularity in the history of
a Catholic Sabbath.

Monday, 25th.—An opportunity offering to-
day, three of us set out on an expedition to
Xeres, a town of Andalusia, from whence
came the Sherry wine formerly so celebrated
in England under the name of *sack.* The

water being too low to carry us over to Port San Maria direct, we proceeded with a fair wind in the long-boat of the Cambrian up the river Guadelete, past the carraccas or dock-yards, &c. We witnessed every where the desolation caused by the late unhappy Revolution: houses unroofed, walls shattered, and the sea-bird flitting round the hearth-stone, proved but too well the contest which had been carried on. The French troops are execrated by the natives, and in more than one instance this dislike was very forcibly expressed: but no wonder! the French are in possession of all authority in the place. Their ships of war lie in the bay, and their troops garrison the town. The customs are entirely under their control, and little is done but by their express permission. They are, however, entitled to much praise. Their conduct is orderly, and they take under their direction the repair of the batteries, which are in imminent danger of becoming a complete ruin, of which the inundation of the town would be one consequence.

The Spaniards are an extraordinary people: with every means of making a vigorous defence, they surrender their liberties, and content themselves with cursing the enslaver. They awaken from a long lethargy to observe the constitution falling, and just ready to crush them in its fall. Instead, however, of applying adequate supports—instead of strenuously labouring to maintain and to strengthen it, they stretch a lingering and reluctant hand beneath: consequently they are ground to powder by the pressure of the superincumbent mass! Their future destiny is a matter of curious speculation. History teaches us not to despair of an event, however distant and improbable. They may yet become a free and a powerful people; for they are naturally high-minded and resolute. Of late, indeed, these characteristics have been depressed and enfeebled; and having become a less moral nation, they are justly, and almost necessarily, less free.

The vices of our own court, during the reign of Charles the Second, enslaved the nation, or at least, retained it in slavery. Never, probably, was greater despotism exhibited, nor ever (for a time) submitted to with less reluctance. The court of France, previous to the

VOL. I.   C

Revolution, was the most debauched in Christendom; slavery could go no further. The mind, debilitated and powerless, shrunk into the most contemptible insignificance; and however desperate and lamentable was the cautery at last applied, it is certain, that nothing but a thorough burning out of the affected parts, could have remedied the evil. Excesses always have attended, and always will attend the Revolution of a long-enslaved nation : the very struggle to burst their bonds asunder is an effort of momentary frenzy; and the sudden snapping of the iron alone serves to hurl the enfranchised being headlong in his course. Then the buoyancy of newly-acquired freedom —the smarting of wounds in which the iron has long festered, are enough to account for, if they do not excuse, the violence of revolutionary licence. These are truths which tyranny would do well to remember. The hour of retribution comes at last; and the longer it is delayed, the more terrible are its operations. The vices of a nation, which are the first promoters and encouragers of slavery, soon become their own bane, openly and effectually : and corruption, once roused by the oppressor's rod, like the scorpion, "girt by fire," plunges into self-destruction. But then anarchy and bloodshed accompany its course. The lightning, which consumes whatsoever obstructs it, purifies the air; and though desolation and death may have marked its progress, they who survive breathe more freely. They have watched it pursuing its awful track of ruin, and their minds expand; their hearts grow chastened, and they learn to substitute gratitude to heaven in the place of scorn,—praises instead of blasphemy. Deeply is the past impressed with the certainty of this. May the present attain to purity by a milder process, and less merited opprobrium!

On reaching Port San Maria, which is also garrisoned by French soldiers, whose shabby equipments surprised us not a little, we heard many anecdotes respecting robberies committed by regularly organized banditti between this town and Xeres. Captain and Mrs. Fox, who had gone thither the preceding day, and returned within half an hour after our arrival, had thought it expedient to procure the guard of three French lancers. They were not,

however, required ; and availing ourselves
of a conveyance which opportunely offered,
we set out without an escort. The fact is,
that Spaniards are marvellously given to
exaggerate trifles into importance ; and, con-
ceiving vividly, throw a strong colouring of
fiction over the most common occurrence.
Aware, in some measure, of this propensity,
we had little hesitation in trusting ourselves
to the chances of the way ; and had no
reason to repent it either in going or in returning.

The country, from Port San Maria to Xeres,
is extremely barren and mountainous, except
on the side toward the sea. Here it is an
entire swamp. A few olive, and occasionally,
orange groves, interrupted the monotony of
the scene, with hedges formed of the aloe, and
a plant called the prickly pear, (the *cactus
opuntia*,) which are almost impenetrable. As
we approached the object of our pilgrimage,
vineyards, of considerable extent, began to
show themselves, but not as in Italy and
France, trained up long poles. The vines
here are not higher than currant bushes, to
which in the distance they have great simi-

larity. The effect is, therefore, less striking
and picturesque. While the fruit, though well
calculated to produce "your excellent Sherris,"
is of inferior flavour, and very small. On reaching Xeres, which is distant about eight miles
from Port San Maria, our coachman, mistaking
the orders we had given him, drove to the
residence of Mr. Gordon, a gentleman of very
extensive mercantile pursuits. Notwithstanding the intrusion, we were received with the
utmost politeness and hospitality; and I am
happy in this opportunity of repeating the
thanks to which himself and his family are so
justly entitled.

. We were shewn the large vaults in which
the house of Gordon and Co. deposit their
wines, capable of containing several thousand
butts. At present the stock consisted of about
fifteen hundred, comprising wines of various
qualities and ages. The quantity of wine
annually made at Xeres, averages very nearly
thirty thousand butts. Of the spoilt wine they
make brandy. The casks are fabricated upon
the premises. When we entered the cooper-
age, the men were dining; and we noticed the
remarkably fine bread of which their meal

partly consisted. A Spaniard, however poor, will eat nothing but the best of its kind ; and supposing him to possess money enough to purchase two articles of an inferior quality, and but *one* of a higher, he will invariably select the last. An Englishman of the same class regards the abundance more than the excellence of his food ; and, enjoying the one, he is little concerned, or at least he is perfectly content to be deprived of the other. This, however, is one of the smallest distinctions between the two nations.

We also visited the wine-vaults of Mr. Cranstoun, which appeared constructed on a better principle than those of Mr. Gordon. They are more airy, and the arrangement is more complete. We tasted a Sherry wine here of the colour of Port, said to have been seventy-five years in the cask. It had a pleasant luscious flavour. Attached to the vaults is a garden of a peculiar formation, but laid out with considerable attention to taste. The beds are usually elevated a considerable height above the paved walk, and bounded by a broad stone border. The walls which surround the garden, are covered with inverted semicircular tiles that catch the rain which falls irregularly and rarely; and thence convey it by narrow tunnels into the beds above mentioned. By this mode, the garden is completely irrigated.

There are several churches in this place. Amongst the rest, the cathedral is a beautiful structure. It is of the Grecian style of architecture, and characterized by more simplicity of ornament than is presented by the religious buildings of Cadiz. There was considerably less glare, and fewer of those ridiculous appendages which disfigure the noble outline of a Catholic building. A number of votive offerings, such as little leaden and waxen heads, legs, arms, and *breasts* *: bunches of rare-coloured ribbons, with much other trumpery, were suspended over an arch.

On the following morning we left Xeres. The English consul, Mr. Brackenbury, this evening gave a ball, to which the officers of the Cambrian were invited. The chief beauties of Cadiz had been collected; and, on the

* In Malta these extraordinary offerings are very common.

whole, there was a sprightly and novel assemblage.   Abundance of French officers were present : of whom the General had the air and manners of an English gentleman.   This was so striking, that it was noticed by most of our party.

The Spanish ladies have not that grace which fancy teaches us to look for.   It might be, that my expectations were too highly raised, or that I had not yet lost the remembrance of my own fascinating countrywomen.   Be this as it may : any one given rout in London, will bring together far more beauty than it seems all Cadiz could furnish.   We were favoured with one or two Spanish songs, by a lady of *purely Spanish origin.*   This last circumstance was announced with no little flourish.   She sang to the piano ; but her voice in my ear was harsh and discordant.   And here I will candidly confess my apprehension, that something of natural prejudice may have followed me from my " father-land."   Not that I am aware of it ; but experiencing so little satisfaction in that which has received a world of high-flown encomium ; and recollecting at the same time how difficult it is to discard at once the feelings which have for years been growing with our growth, I am a little inclined to suspect my impartiality.

CHAPTER II.

WEDNESDAY, 27*th Oct.*—This morning we put to sea; but, in consequence of a calm, made little way.

Thursday, 28th Oct.—A breeze springing up during the night, about six o'clock we stood off the Rock of Gibraltar. Captain Hamilton sent out a boat to ascertain, whether by touching there we should run the risk of quarantine at Malta; but the very vague answer which was returned, determined him to proceed. There was, therefore, no opportunity to gratify our curiosity by an examination of this celebrated fortress.

Friday, 29th Oct. — The morning being perfectly calm, we remained long in sight of Gibraltar. It lay beautifully encircled in a white wreath of mist, upon which the sun glanced, imparting to it the delicate hue of the plum, when it lies sleeping in the morning dew. About six o'clock, P. M. a Sardinian schooner of war hove in sight. The Cambrian hoisted her colours; but the signal was not returned. Captain Hamilton directed a gun to be fired at her : still she slighted the warning, and a second ball, aimed with more precision, struck the water at no great distance from the bow, while our frigate put about in pursuit. A third shot, however, had the desired effect;—the national flag was hoisted, and we left her to continue her course. The obstinacy of the Sardinian commander was as remarkable as it was unadvised ; and might have been productive of the most unpleasant consequences.

Tuesday, 2d Nov.—A British merchant brig, not lowering her top-sails according to Act of Parliament relating to marine matters, was fired at with a musket. At last, a boat being sent out, the master excused himself under the plea of ignorance ; and in truth, from all accounts, he was its absolute personification. He had come from Smyrna.

Saturday, 6th Nov.—Passed the little island

of Galeta this morning about ten o'clock.   It
is a barren rock, and apparently the effect of a
volcanic eruption.   The coral fishers use it as
a station, and here leave their wives and children while they pursue their adventurous mode
of life.   At other times a few goats are the
only habitants.

Monday, 8th Nov.—Arrived at Malta late
at night.

Wednesday, 10th Nov.—We are to sail this
evening, and the short period of our stay has
prevented me from examining with accuracy
this very remarkable island.   I shall therefore
content myself with a cursory description, in-
asmuch as many opportunities, I am told, will
occur, for a more minute inspection.   We are
to return here every six months.

Malta and the adjacent islands of Gozo and
Comeno (which for the present I shall pass)
have a singularly barren and unprepossessing
outline.   They are solely rocks, without one
single prospect of verdure as they are beheld
from the sea : when examined internally they
improve but little.   The great value of these
places arises from their situation in the Medi-
terranean, and the impregnable fortresses which

they form. The harbours of La Valetta * may be termed natural excavations of the solid rock, and are secure and convenient basins. The houses rise on each side one above another, being built upon the declivity of the rock with the stone hewn from it; this is a kind of free-stone, extremely soft and porous. The streets are for the most part remarkably precipitous, but the houses are regular and uniform, square built, and in some instances white-washed, with wooden balconies projecting from the higher part. They have commonly iron gratings over the lower windows, and in this, as in other instances, reminded me of Cadiz, *especially* in the intolerable smell of garlick which mostly issues from them. The fortifications excel probably every thing of the kind, and though they deserve the utmost attention, are of too technical a character for description.

The governor's palace (once that of the grand masters) is a large building. It exhibits some very beautiful specimens of ancient tapestry, and a number of paintings by the first artists, principally, however, portraits of

* La Valetta is the metropolis of Malta.

the grand masters of the order of St. John of
Jerusalem.   The armoury is an extensive apartment, comprehending the whole length of one
side of the square.   Here are upwards of seventeen thousand stand of arms, besides a great
variety of ancient weapons which belonged to
the knights of St. John.   Three suits of mail
armour worn by Wevercourt, a celebrated
grand master (of whom there are many portraits), are reposited in this place ; one of them
is inlaid with gold, and in this he is usually
represented.

The church of St. John is a magnificent
building, though somewhat the worse for the
various mutations of fortune which it has seen.
The walls and ceiling are of carved work gilded
throughout.   The pavement is wholly composed
of monumental insignia described by vari-
coloured marbles ; and there is an inlaid altar-
screen of the same materials, but representing
wreaths of flowers, &c. of the most exquisite
order.   The tombs of the grand masters are
scattered about the building ; they are of
beautiful workmanship, and well deserving inspection.   An embossed silver railing before
an oratory here was saved from the rapacious

hands of Buonaparte only by stratagem.   It was painted in imitation of wood, and thus escaped the crucible.   The outward structure of this building is oddly, not to say grotesquely contrived.

The public library of Malta contains many thousand volumes, and is in a progressive state of improvement: there are, however, few manuscripts, and the printed volumes are almost entirely modern editions.

The opera-house is a poor affair, and the music and acting, so far as I am able to judge, many degrees worse.

Thursday, 11th Nov.—Early this morning we set sail for Naples, under a quarantine of ten days, including the voyage.   The wind has been unfavourable, and such delay is not to be regretted, since it will shorten the term of our imprisonment when we arrive.

Friday, 12th Nov.—This morning afforded us a first glimpse of Mount Etna, at a distance of about forty miles.   We observed it during the day emitting volumes of smoke, but there was no visible flame.   As night approached we were driven over to the coast of Calabria,

10

which exhibited its bold and rocky shore in all
the solemnity of a serene twilight.

Saturday, 13*th Nov.*——Towards evening we
stood nearer to Etna, which presented a most
magnificent appearance.   The whole mountain
was of an intense blue, save that a broad belt
of white clouds girded its centre; presently
they ascended to the summit, and formed
themselves into a wreath, one point of which
touched the apex of the mountain, resembling
the circle of thin smoke vulgarly termed a
shroud, which arises sometimes from a burning candle.   This gradually died away as the
night advanced, and was soon lost in the shadowy outline of the volcano.   A momentary
gleam of fire shot up after the night set in, but
it was not again discoverable.

Sunday, 14*th Nov.*——We entered the strait
called the Faro di Messina at an early hour.
The mountains on each side were enveloped in
purple mist, and crowned with white fleecy
clouds.   As day increased these last assumed
a brighter tinge, while the sun's rays thrown
across the eastern barrier of the mountains, coloured the dark pile opposite with a rosy hue.

The loftier clouds changed successively into red, yellow, and gold, and at last disappeared before the full splendour of a Southern sun. A delicious prospect opened upon us, which continued through the day. The strait is about seven miles broad, and high mountains frowning upon each other from its confronting sides, sometimes in shade, and sometimes glittering in light, amid a multitude of more diminutive objects, were distinguished by their solemn magnificence. Here and there, seated upon a commanding eminence, was the house of a peasant, surrounded by the olive and fig-tree. At the foot of the mountain, reposing picturesquely upon the sea-shore, groups of fishermens' cottages, and occasionally a town of some magnitude, presented themselves; and as the wind was contrary, indeed almost approaching to a calm, we were under the necessity of tacking from shore to shore : thus an opportunity occurred of gratifying our curiosity in a greater degree than would otherwise have been possible. On the Sicilian coast Messina appeared to much advantage : a portion of the inhabitants were employed in fishing for the tunny as we passed, but apparently their suc-

cess did not equal their exertions. Captain
Smyth has given a description of the method
by which it is caught. The water-courses on
these mountains seem to be very numerous,
and in truth, at certain parts of the year, the
towns at their feet must suffer greatly from the
violence of the torrent.

The whole of this day was employed in
working out of the strait. We twice reached
the Faro Point and were drawn back by
the current, of which the celebrated SCYLLA,
is, I presume, to bear the blame. The vortex
of Charybdis, situated just beyond the Mole of
Messina, is described by mariners as being in
some respects dangerous, but I do not find that
this is thought to be the case with Scylla,
The distance between them is nearly six miles,
and if these be indeed the points indicated by
so many classical descriptions, I am totally at
a loss to conceive how the frailest bark should
run any danger of the one while it avoided the
other. But a country so liable to mutation
must needs have undergone the most extraordinary changes; and it is perhaps owing to
the difficulty of assigning more appropriate situations, that these have been fixed on as the

likeliest sites, and denominated accordingly. The volcano of Stromboli was seen indistinctly as we passed the Faro Point.

Wednesday, 17th *Nov.*—About two o'clock A.M. we anchored in the Bay of Naples, and have to-day remained in quarantine. We are to continue so till Friday. The Bay has long been an object of encomium, and description has exercised sufficiently both the pen and the pencil—it is, however, uncommonly beautiful. Behind us lies Capri, celebrated for the country residences of Augustus and Tiberius Cæsar. To the right Vesuvius rears its giant form covered with vineyards " as with a garment." The town of Portici reposes at its foot, its white houses shining in the sun, and scattered like a flock of sheep along the coast. In front rise the Appennines, looking down upon a segment of the Bay, upon which stands part of the Neapolitan capital ; and on the left, rising along the whole side of a mountainous tract, and surmounted by a citadel, the main portion is situated, at this moment glimmering in the twilight with ten thousand lights. The Revenge, bearing the admiral's flag, is at present in the Bay ; besides the Seringapatam, Captain

Southerby; and a Neapolitan frigate. At sunset Mount Vesuvius wore a delicious aspect—but of this hereafter. Although it is my intention to touch but slightly subjects so hacknied and threadbare, yet I ought not altogether to omit one of the most surprizing of natural phenomena.

Thursday, 18th Nov.—This morning we were entertained by a couple of musicians who rowed their boat to the ship. They made a singular appearance; one of them was arrayed in a jelly-bag sort of cap, terminating in a tassel. His long coarse hair curled upon his shoulders, and gave a ludicrous but characteristic air to his lank countenance; a sheep-skin coat, with the wool outward, a pair of dark cloth galligaskins " all rags and tatters," with worsted hosen wrinkling into as many lines as a " new Map o' the Indies," completed his costume. He played the bag-pipes, the bag of which was composed of the undressed skin of a goat or kid in its original shape and length, of which one leg was employed to conduct the wind from the mouth into the lower regions. The pipes of this instrument were like the " masts of some high ammiral," and truly he supplied them with many a hurricane. His comrade wore a conical-shaped hat, a Mount Vesuvius, and blew lustily "an oaten reed." The remainder of his dress resembled that of his companion, save that his nether garment was of a cerulean plush, a venerable piece of antiquity, probably from Herculaneum or Pompeii —about this, however, I was never satisfied. They obtained a few small pieces of money and retired, doubtless well pleased with the power of their music.

Friday, 19th Nov.—We are still in quarantine, very greatly to our annoyance. This is the birth-day of one of the Neapolitan royal family; the guns of the batteries, and of the men of war in the bay are firing :—we understand that it is considered a great holiday. This circumstance adds to our mortification. The king holds a levee, and I had hoped, by means of a letter of introduction which I bring to the English ambassador, to have been presented at court ; however, I must bear the disappointment as I may. We have just heard that the quarantine will last till Sunday.

Sunday, 21st Nov.—After service to-day we were landed at the Vittoria Hotel, near the Villa

Reale, into which we immediately hastened.
This is a public walk, in fact the *Alameyda* of
Naples. It is planted with a variety of trees
on each side, and ornamented with a number
of statues. In the centre of the walk, as you
enter, is a fine group of statuary representing
Dirce about to be tied to a bull which the sons
of Antiope have seized by the horns. The
animal deserves particular attention : it is an
antique of exquisite workmanship. The rest
of the group are modern ; so are the legs of
the bull. The walks began to fill soon after
our arrival, and to exhibit a gay aspect. The
vast number of military costumes in Naples
surprizes a stranger, every regiment appearing
differently arrayed. This was in some measure accounted for by the information that ten
thousand Austrian troops are garrisoned in the
city and neighbourhood. Still the variety is
immense, and might almost seem left to the
inclination of every fantastic individual. The
tyros of the military colleges also are set forth
cap-a-pee in regimental uniform, and brought
hither on Sunday to parade, attended by their
pedagogue, a dirty-looking *padre* in his huge
three-cornered hat ; and who, contrasted with

blue coats and scarlet shoulder-knots, with the scarlet tufts of the youngsters' caps, resembles a scare-crow in a field that *should* have produced wheat, but of which the major portion is hare-bells and cockle.

After walking in the Villa Reale for some time, we proceeded to inspect the city itself, " qui est si animée et si oisive tout à la fois." The streets were very crowded and very dirty, and the loud nasal cry of the venders of certain esculent articles was incessant ; let the reader add to this the rattling of hundreds of fiacres, hurrying violently along the narrow streets of the Neapolitan metropolis, and he will form some idea of the confused but lively scene which was presented to us.   The only tolerably good street is the Strada de Toledo, running in a line with the royal palaces, and containing some of the public buildings of Naples, such as the Real Muséo Borbonico and the offices of the Finance Department.   We returned about two o'clock to the Villa Reale, where the military band was playing.   The number of carriages which passed the promenade reminded me of Hyde Park on a Sunday evening.   But here *all* the inhabitants poured forth in tor-

rents, "tag, rag and bob-tail;" people of all
ranks were taking a Sabbath's airing : and this
forms the chief distinction between the assembled population of London and Naples.
The lower class are not separated from the
higher ; nor while the gentry enjoy the fresco
of the evening are the tradesmen prohibited
the same enjoyment in the same place.   Thus
there is a more national character in the scene ;
the different grades of society are not so invidiously distinguished, and the hired fiacre of
the venditore del maccheroni jogs along after
the carriage of an Italian prince or princess,
(such as they are !) without censure and without
fear.   I allude to the exclusion of hackney ve-
hicles from Hyde Park ; but I admit that if it
were otherwise the crowd would be too great,
and that much of the interest and splendour of
the scene would be considerably diminished.
Perhaps also there might be some danger in
augmenting the concourse of a London populace : but nothing of all this seems to occur at
Naples; and it is extremely diverting to notice
the marked physiognomy and emphatic ges-
ticulation of the lower order of Italians as
they pass along.   They seem so happy and yet

so squalid and miserable, with so much of civilization, and yet with so little idea of it, or care for it. In one place you observe a dozen persons, male and female, crowded into a narrow carriage, the women without bonnets, and their black hair (surmounted commonly by a silver comb) straggling about the eyes and ears. In the latter stick immense rings, often broader than a crown-piece, and I should think as heavy. The bright and dark eyes of these damsels impart a singular expression to their dingy features, and give an odd, and rather disagreeable, effect to the contour of the face. Very generally a child wrapped up like a mummy is conveyed upon the bosom. A ragged and dirty fellow, in a sugar-loaf hat, jumps up behind, overlooking fellows within equally ragged and dirty :——thus they set forth. In another place are two or three priests " in cloth of brown that erst was black," holding the reins of a calesse, while on a step in the rear stands the driver, (and proprietor perhaps) with a whip, which he applies as necessity dictates to the steed in front, flourishing it magnificently over the heads of the clerical party within. Then again there is a kind of vehicle which is made to contain but one, gilded and carved, with a pole standing at the stern, by which the flagellator of the steed maintains his not very enviable situation. And then——but hold, " I'll see no more :" dinner calls, and a " *civet de sanglier*" already smokes upon the board.

Monday, 22d Nov.——Immediately after breakfast, we set out upon an expedition to Pompeii. The roads were intolerably dusty, for being composed solely of lava, and no attention paid to sweeping, the passenger is overwhelmed with a continual cloud. Besides this, our carriage was beset by troops of deformed and diseased beggars, who, being for the most part blind, were led by stout boys, and ran by our side uttering the most doleful and discordant cries. The number of Lazzaroni which former travellers notice in the streets of Naples has considerably diminished, and many disgusting sights are consequently prevented. But the suburbs and roads leading to the principal objects of curiosity are still overrun with them. Nor is their pertinacity the least surprizing. They continue upon a long trot by the side of the vehicle, burdened as they are with all their diseases, (though part are no doubt impostures) for a great distance, and generally accomplish by this indomitable perseverance the object of their desires. Travellers are glad to free themselves from the uproar, at whatever rate.

About twelve English miles from Naples stands Pompeii, certainly the most remarkable remnant of antiquity that now exists. So much has already been said respecting these ruins, and so much that is worthy of remembrance, that it may seem a work of mere supererogation to enter into a detailed account. The road has become so beaten, and has justly been a matter of such intense and minute curiosity, that we have scarcely an alternative in our power. But the mind here will never be satiated : it must recur again and again, with augmented delight, to an object which plays so luxuriantly around the imagination, and seizes, in its powerful grasp, the best and most fascinating visions of the heart. For this reason, although it would be useless to describe systematically a place which a multitude of celebrated antiquaries have laboriously, and, for the most part, accurately dissected, yet I cannot withstand the temptation of advderting in general terms to the impression which the sight of Pompeii made upon my feelings; and of endeavouring to interest the reader, not merely with the place itself, (for that interest he must long ago have experienced,) but with the pilgrimage of the humble individual who now ventures to obtrude on his attention.

It does not appear generally known, or, at least, it has not been generally noticed, that the honour of discovering these singular ruins is due to the proprietor of a vineyard which then stood on the spot. He was about to plant an additional number of vines on an unoccupied division of his farm; and the first blow of the mattock, while it repelled and impeded his efforts, stimulated curiosity, and at length gave birth to a town! This happened a little more than sixty years ago.

It is to be lamented, that the traveller now has not the advantage which was at first open to him. The paintings, the houshold utensils, the skeletons of those who were consumed in the bursting out of the mountain, are all removed. We see, indeed, the places they occupied : the impression of certain drinking-cups, the ruts of carriage-wheels, and the marks of a cord upon the margin of a well, nay, the very scrawls which the soldiers of a Roman legion made to amuse themselves during the hours of their watch ; but that which would have given life to the inanimate and deathly stillness of the place,—which would have aided the excursions of imagination, and embodied the winged conceptions that dart through the obscurity of past time, and fix themselves in all the vivid colourings of truth—these are wanting. They have been removed to the museum at Naples : and though nothing assuredly can deprive them of the charms with which such high antiquity has encrusted them, it is easy to understand the loss occurring to the imagination, as well as pleasure to the heart. It has been alleged, that were they to retain their original situation, they would be purloined : and it has been said, on the other hand, that a guard of soldiers, whose time at present is occupied by gambling and debauchery, would easily secure the smaller antiquities of Pompeii from depredation. But this may be questioned : the constant attention requisite would speedily weary the inert Neapolitan; and a guard of Austrians could be but for a limited period. Besides, there would not be wanting those upon whom bribery has its effect; and thus would vanish in a moment what no event might hereafter replace. Moreover, the action of the air upon many of these frail relics, snatched, and barely snatched, from destruction, would operate materially. So that in a short time, that which the fire was unable totally to ruin, exposure to the elements would effect. Still there have been discoveries made here which would receive little injury, would be guarded with little risk, and add powerfully to the feeling with which we consider this remarkable depository of Roman magnificence. Let the drinking-glasses, which are liable to be broken, remain in their present custody; let the cameos, gems, and engraved stones, the wheat, barley, acorns, and grains of all descriptions, which have been found here, be preserved in Naples, together with whatever else may be considered fragile, whether from its nature or diminutive size; but surely the skeletons might have retained their post, ornamented with the least

15

valuable bracelets with which they were discovered : the earthen amphoræ would have
received no detriment, nor would many of the
statues have been worse for standing as they
were found.   Part of the kitchen utensils, such
as kettles, pipkins, baking-pans, frying-pans
for eggs, &c. &c. might have been left ; and
out of 635 weights, measures, scales, steel-
yards, lamps, and chandeliers *, surely a few
dozen might have been spared for public gratification, as they were originally disposed. To
these might have been added, the original
seats; and *one* particular room carefully locked
up and examined through a glass case, or by
express permission of the government in writing
without this obstruction, containing the whole
apparatus of a lady's toilette.   In Pompeii
were found, says the Abbe Romanelli, " bracelets of gold, ear-rings, necklaces, chains of
gold, rings set with precious stones, gold and
silver bodkins, galloons of real gold, tooth and
ear-picks, scissars, needles, ivory spindles, and
all manner of trinkets; nay, those very same

* " Il numero di detti oggetti ascende a quello di
635," says " La Guida per lo Real Museo Borbonico."

things that mended the defects of nature—
false teeth, wigs, false eye-brows, odoriferous
waters, ointments, perfumes and rouge, which
they called *purpurissum*, in small crystal
phials." How delightful it would have been,
and what a spell it must have thrown around
the whole place, to see, although through "a
crystal medium," this curious scene! Where
is she for whom the preparation is made?
Has she proceeded to the bath, arrayed in the
loose floating garment to which Roman dames
on these occasions were accustomed? Observe
how that metal mirror shines, as though even
in the absence of its owner it reflected back
some portion of its borrowed beauty. Where
are her tire-women—her *cosmetæ?* why do
they not hasten to their duty? her head-gear
lies uncurled and loose; her eye-brows are un-
smoothed; and her teeth, heaven help us! will
be distinguished by the eagle-eye of the inquisitive lover. Hark! she comes; I hear the
rustling of her garments, and the Roman virgin
will presently appear in all her *classic* dignity!
Alas! such dreams would be dissipated by very
different objects. The rags of some itinerant
lazzaroni might occupy the image which

the flowing folds of ancient costume had elicited ; and a putrifying sore surrounded with coagulated filth, like Vesuvius amid its lava, would be presented for the fresh glowing countenance of a youthful maiden, just emancipated from the luxury of the bath.

In one of the Arabian tales, we have an account of a whole city turned suddenly into stone. Every thing remains in its original position, — " lifeless, but life-like." " Les peintures, les bronzes étaient encore dans leur beauté première, et tout ce qui peut servir aux usages domestiques est conservé d'une manière effrayante. Les amphores sont encore préparées pour le festin du jour suivant ; la farine qui allait être pétrie est encore là : les restes d'une femme sont encore ornés des parures qu'elle portait dans le jour de fête, que le volcan a troublé, et ses bras desséchés ne remplissent plus le bracelet des pierreries qui les entoure encore *."

Whether Madame de Stael ever witnessed Pompeii in the state here described, and in which it doubtless was, is a matter for question.

* Corrinna.

It seems probable, that the particulars alluded to would be removed the moment they were discovered. But certainly it is Pompeii, so described, or so seen, that might have given rise to the fiction in the Arabian tales. And in seeing the desolation of the Roman city, we have the best possible conception not only of it, but of the petrified city in Upper Egypt, mentioned in Perry's " View of the Levant," where it is said, many statues of men and women are at this day to be seen. This, perhaps, is the origin of the Arabian figment.

It has been asserted by Dion Cassius, a Roman historian, who flourished about a century and a half after the destruction of Herculaneum and Pompeii, by the eruption of Mount Vesuvius, that the inhabitants of one or both of the above-mentioned cities were overwhelmed by the lava-flood as they witnessed a theatrical representation. This is considered by Mr. Eustace as so palpable an absurdity, that it is difficult to conceive how the historian could relate it with so much gravity. The reasons are, that the first agitation united to the threatening aspect of the mountain, must have banished all inclination for mirth; that

the number of skeletons discovered among the
ruins, does not bear out the supposition, and
that it may even be questioned, whether one
skeleton was found in or near the theatre. I
will not urge, in this place, the truth of that
ancient maxim, "Quem Deus vult perdere
prius dementat," but I will ask, whether the
reiterated warnings of approaching destruction
were sufficient to admonish JERUSALEM of its
fate? If the first commotions of the earth
produced, as we know they did, little real injury; if the smoke and partial emissions of
flame—or admit it to have been lava—occasioned in the first instance no positive or
general harm, we know well enough that the
indications, however terrible, would lose their
terror through the frequency of the occurrence,
and the throb of apprehension subside into
comparative security. Mr. Eustace remarks,
(and admitting the fact, I should draw from
it a different inference,) that the inhabitants
of this country were not then accustomed to
volcanic phenomena. An earthquake, however, sixteen years previously, overthrew part of
the town, which they then rebuilt; and might
at the same time have acquired some insight

E 2

into the cause and the consequence. But
granting that they were ignorant of both,
surely this very circumstance would contribute
to lull them the more into inertness ! During
a cessation of the convulsed and agitated state
of the mountain, they might have sought to
lose the remembrance of their solicitude in the
mimicry of the stage, and, in such a moment,
have been hurried to their graves ! The very
multitude compressed closely together in the
last desperate effort to escape, would, when
the fiery mass surprised them, promote their
own dissolution : and the concavity of the
theatre receiving into its bosom a more than
common share of the ignited particles, must
also have aided a calcination, which the weight
of the superincumbent strata reduced at length
to powder. This would account, I think, very
satisfactorily for the small number of skeletons
which have been found : though let it be remembered, that in all probability not above
one-third of the city has been uncovered. The
excavations which are now going on, prove
this to demonstration ; and, but two months
ago, a splendid bath, about which the workmen were busy when I visited Pompeii, was

opened. It is very large, and built in the form of a dome. In the centre is a beautiful font, and around the margin an inscription, of which I regret that my haste led to an incorrect copy. Several other discoveries have also been made : the one I allude to stands near the Pantheon.

But there are several other circumstances, for which nothing but this sudden, this instantaneous obstruction of life can account. In a villa, (supposed, by the way, to be Cicero's,) having a cellar beneath, were found a number of large amphoræ, and about twenty skeletons. Into this vault the unhappy creatures had rushed on ascertaining, by some means which we cannot now understand, that the torrent had overtaken them. Here they must have been suffocated, and hence the preservation of their bones. There is a house on the left-hand as you proceed from the residence of the guide, at the most distant point from the theatres ; upon the threshold of which appears, in Mosaic, the word " SALVE." Before this house were discovered several skeletons, one of them held a lamp in its bony fingers, and all of them something, perhaps some article of household use : what but the suddenness of the storm could have produced so singular a position? The heat of the ashes would here be less; for there would probably be a freer passage for the air, while the distance from the source of the eruption is greater. In the state I have mentioned, numbers of skeletons were dug up —the greater part standing, and in the very posture in which they had expired.

But of all, curious as they are, that most deserving attention, in my mind, is the Amphitheatre of Pompeii. It is in admirable repair, and capable of containing upwards of thirty thousand spectators. It has a wonderfully imposing appearance, and cannot fail most sensibly to affect the mind. Mr. Hamilton, our ambassador at Naples, informed me, that he has frequently seen tears gush from the eyes of those who have regarded this magnificent spectacle of desolation for the first time—and I am not surprized at it. This immense structure was once peopled with eager and ardent life; on this very arena the dying gladiator " breathed his sullen soul away;" and here the Retiarii foiled or succumbed before the arts of their desperate antagonists.

13

Barbarous as these sports were, they are identified with the national character ; and standing on the loftiest point of the amphitheatre, who can look down without emotion upon the spot where such savage contests for life and death were carried on——where the blood of the captive was inhumanly poured forth to satiety upon the thirsty sand ; and where pleasure lighted even the female eye, (strange power of custom!) as the victor received the plaudits of the assembled multitude? And who can gaze upon the vacant and broken seats before him, nor turn to the appalling shout, which, in the moment of victory, thirty thousand voices raised to heaven? voices which were soon to sink down into the tremulous whisper of despair, and which long ago have ceased their murmur! What a contrast does the picture present——the sinewy arm then waved in acclamation is now an impalpable powder, or, at most, a carious bone! The haughty brow is humbled, and the stately form then enfolded in the toga, hath neither existence nor a name!

These reflections, however common, and however tame, powerfully impress themselves on the mind. To withhold them were almost like suspending the respiration, they rise spontaneously with the breath, and demand articulation. But I hasten to quit a place around which I have perhaps lingered too long, but which I quit with the greatest reluctance. This was not however the case with my companions, and may not be with my readers; one of the former protested that he had seen much better ruins in England, all ruins were alike, and he knew very well what was to be seen here—but then to have been at Naples without *saying* that he had seen Pompeii was intolerable—to be unable to tell his friends that he had *seen* a place which all the world sees, was not to be thought of. He therefore posts to Pompeii—posts through it—eats and drinks, and returns. And this, I firmly believe, comprized the whole of his information on the subject.

> " Œstuat ingens
> Imo in corde pudor, mixtoque insania luctu."

We returned somewhat late in the evening to Naples, and I hastened to make preparations for accompanying his excellency, the English ambassador, to a rout at Lady Drummond's. The rooms were crowded, and her ladyship played the obliging hostess *à mer-veilles*. Out of four hundred visitors not more than sixty were English, and the majority of the males were naval and military officers, who sparkled in all the magnificence of stars and embroidery. There was a general who figured away at the age of a hundred, and consider-ably resembled, it seemed to me, our late ex-cellent sovereign; his name I have forgot. Many beautiful Neapolitan women were pre-sent, among whom the Princess Tercazi, in my humble opinion, far exceeded the rest: she has a very sweetly expressive face,

> " A pleasant smiling cheek, a speaking eye,
> A brow for love to banquet royally,"—

and a good deal of that naïveté of manner which is so engaging to foreigners. Of her private character I have nothing to say, for I know nothing, save that she is nineteen years of age and has five children! Proh Jupiter!

Amongst the number of pretty nothings which were uttered this evening, I overheard a French lady compliment a gentleman upon the recovery of his good looks, which, it seems, had been " *dérangés*" by a late illness; " *Ah !*"

cried he tenderly, " *c'est la réflexion de votre image !*" meaning, if it comprehended a meaning, that he was her mirror; and that in regarding him she beheld purely the reflected lustre of her own charms.   A pretty method of complimenting himself, for which the lady in question seemed not over and above thankful.   She smiled with some apparent exertion, waved her hand, and retreated.   Quadrilles, waltzes, and cotillions were the order of the evening; and, on the whole, the dark glittering eyes of the Neapolitan women, contrasted with their sombre dresses, and the gay uniforms of the military, formed a splendid and interesting scene.

CHAPTER III.

TUESDAY, *23d Nov.*—To-day I made the tour of the Bourbonic Museum, in which the contents of Herculaneum and Pompeii, &c. &c. have been deposited. Amongst other things an exquisite bust of Caracalla, two feet and a half high, particularly delighted me : there is great expression in the face, and the disposition of the hair is admirable. A full length statue of Aristides in the act of haranguing, and Silenus intoxicated and reclining on a skin of wine, are each in their way delicious specimens of ancient sculpture ; they were found in Herculaneum. Indeed, the statuary brought from this place alone is very extensive, and will afford many an hour of rich gratification.

In another part of the museum is preserved a vast variety of grain in the different states, discovered in Herculaneum, besides a burnt

loaf of bread eight inches and a half in dia-
meter marked

ERISQCRANI..... RISER.....

This inscription, whatever it may imply, reminds one of the present practice of marking
gingerbread and cakes.   There are also snares,
threads, and a bird-net—probably such as
Horace mentions in the second ode of the
fifth book—

> " Amite levi *rara* tendit *retia*,
>   Turdis edacibus dolos ;
> Pavidumve leporem, et advenam *laqueo* gruem,
>   Jucunda captat prœmia."

And what is not the least curious, there is a
quantity of linen cloth found in the washing-
tub.

In a painter's shop at Pompeii was discovered a pot of verde antique of an earthy character, and probably amalgamated with some
mineral.

Two bronze seats, exactly similar to our
garden chairs, deserve attention : with a number of helmets, cuirasses, spears, quivers, &c.
&c. used both by the Greeks and Romans.   A

considerable quantity of rouge, metal looking-glasses, distaffs, ivory pins and bodkins, surgeons' instruments, &c. are arranged in tolerable order. Nearly three thousand Grecian vases have been collected, of which many are extremely beautiful. Of the picture galleries no mention is necessary; they contain the workmanship of the first artists in the world, and have been perhaps sufficiently illustrated by members of the fraternity. The most curious, and to many the most interesting, part of this collection will be the Papyri or ancient manuscripts found in the library of a disciple of Epicurus at Herculaneum, during the last century; they have the appearance of charcoal, and were so considered when originally met with. The account given of this discovery at Naples is, that on continuing the excavation an ink-stand and a number of pens were turned up, together with two or more bronze busts of Epicurus, whose name was thereon engraven: hence, concluding that the place in question was a library, by the assistance of one Antonio Piaggio, a monk, the Papyri were unrolled, although with extreme difficulty. The following is given as the process, but I am unable to vouch for its authenticity, circumstances having prevented me from inspecting it.

" At the bottom of a glass box are fixed two metal screws inserted in a like number of semicircular plates, on which the roll of Papyrus is placed in an horizontal direction. These screws are used to raise or depress the Papyrus.

" The roll being placed upon the semicircular plates, and the beginning ascertained by means of incisions made as it revolves, threads are run through it and fastened to the upper part of the box, which support and draw up the Papyrus as it is gradually unfolded. In this state gold-beaters' leaf is applied to the back of the writing moistened with isinglass of more or less consistency, as the case may require. Thus strengthened, the unrolled Papyrus is drawn up, and when the surface of one page is found to adhere to another it is disengaged by means of a pointed iron. This process is continued till the whole be developed.

" In this situation it is spread over a small table, and an exact engraving is immediately taken. The defective parts are then supplied, avoiding every alteration of the original, and undergoing a minute inspection by competent persons appointed for that purpose. It is now sent to the press, and afterwards translated into Latin; the defective parts being carefully filled up and distinguished by red ink."

About four hundred and eight of these Papyri have been unfolded, and of these eighty-eight are legible throughout, the rest are fragments. In the year 1793 two volumes were published, the one containing a work on music, by Philodemus, (probably a writer of licentious verses in the time of Cicero,) and the other a fragment of a Latin Poem of uncertain date. A third volume is either published or about to issue from the press. The unsuccessful result of Sir Humphrey Davy's efforts in unrolling the Papyri is well known.

The library is said to contain 180,000 printed volumes, (but I doubt the accuracy of this information) and nearly five thousand manuscripts, amongst which is one of Tasso, and another of no less a personage than *Saint* Thomas Aquinas.

In the evening of this day we went to the theatre of San Carlos. It is certainly decorated with great splendour, and not without some taste. The scenery is excellent, as well as the music: respecting the rest I am silent. The king was present, a long, thin, and venerable personage, with powdered hair, and four or five stars glittering upon his sober suit of black. The Duke of Calabria sat in an adjoining box.

Wednesday, 24th Nov.—About ten o'clock I set out with a companion for Vesuvius, though the day was extremely unpromising: but we thought it better to avail ourselves of the first opportunity, rather than lose altogether the sight of one of the most magnificent spectacles in nature. Arriving at Portici, a town built upon the ruins of Herculaneum, we obtained asses and a guide. The ascent is by a watercourse, and greatly obstructed by the large pieces of broken lava which the torrent has left. We arrived at the hermitage about one o'clock, and were met by a "jolly friar," who invited us into his mansion. This we declined, for our coachman mistaking his orders carried us at least three miles beyond the place of ascent; we had therefore no time to lose, and accordingly hastened up the mountain with all celerity. A little beyond the hermitage is a wooden cross, to which, at Pentecost, all Naples marches in procession : here a feast is held, and perhaps it is to this " work of mens' hands" that the prayer of the Catholic arises, accompanied, it may be, by that curious specimen of idolatrous bigotry of which Bishop Hall has preserved a copy.   It is well worth transcription.

" HYMNUS AD CRUCEM.

" Ara crucis,
Lampas lucis,
Sola salus hominum :
Nobis pronum,
Fac patronum,
Quem tulisti dominum."

At this time the summit of Mount Vesuvius was enveloped in clouds, and though our guide assured us that they would disperse before we had climbed so high, yet it was all along exceedingly doubtful.   In fact they did not ; and all our labour, all the pain of the ascent was not remunerated even by a transient glimpse of the bay and country of Naples.   The crater of the volcano was filled with mist, and the whole cone was shrouded with a very thick cloud.   Thus situated, it was thought best to

make our way down as fast as possible, for the
dew began to penetrate our clothes, while a
strong wind loosed the tufo from the apex of
the mountain, and blew it with considerable
violence into our eyes. I had no idea of the
difficulty of the ascent, and was glad, even with
all these disadvantages, to seat myself on the
edge of the crater. As we descended the rain
began, and before we returned to the house
of Salvatori (our guide) we were completely
drenched. He desired us to insert our names
in a book kept for that purpose, and various
were the comments, and as various the languages, that we met with. The best of our
wetting was, that it introduced us to the wife
and children of our guide, who were as fine a
specimen of Neapolitan beauty as I have seen.
A lovely child of four or five years lay in the
cradle ill of the typhus fever, and another
of thirteen or fourteen, full of sprightliness
and simplicity, busied herself in aiding our
attempts to dry our clothes; while the mother, who must have been a fine woman in her
day, vigorously wafted a chafing-dish with the
bottom of her petticoat! The room was hung
round with tolerable paintings in oil of several

members of the royal family, which Salvatori
informed us he had purchased at Naples. After
swallowing a cordial glass of *annisette*, we got
into our carriage and drove rapidly back.   In
the evening we were present at the representation of Acis and Galatea, in the Opera del
Fondo, and retired to our quarters with no
other effect of the journey than fatigue.

Thursday, 25th Nov.—The rain fell violently all the morning, and the water " rushed
like a torrent" down the slopes of the streets.
I contrived, however, to get up to the citadel of
St. Elmo, a strong fortress upon a high rock
which commands the town.   It is garrisoned
by Austrian troops, and is curious from being
principally cut through the solid rock, as from
the winding and precipitous paths which lead
to it.   The view from the summit is fine, extending over the city and country of Naples,
the bay, Appennines, &c. &c.

Friday, 26th Nov.—It being determined
that we should return on board the Cambrian
this afternoon, a short excursion to Puzzuoli,
the ancient Puteoli, was proposed and acceded
to ; in consequence of which we set forth about
ten o'clock in the morning, and passed through

a most singular excavation of rock three quarters of a mile long and from seventy to eighty
feet high, called the Grotto of Posilippo, where
Madame de Staël tells us " des milliers de
Lazzaroni passent leur vie, en sortant seule-
ment à midi *pour voir le soleil,* et dormant le
reste du jour, pendant que leurs femmes filent."
By which it would seem that they never eat,
though they may *dream* of eating, but subsist
on sunshine and sleep.   However, I saw nothing of it.   In this place is the tomb of Virgil.
We traversed a rich country, the road lying
through vineyards, which now began to exhibit
the fall of the leaf.   Reaching the sea-shore,
we wound along huge rocks, all more or less
consecrated by legends of other days.   The
promontory of Misenus and the Lucrine lake
are at no great distance ; and a little beyond
Puzzuoli is Baiæ, so celebrated for its baths
and the luxury and lasciviousness of which
it once was the scene.   Our time was too limited to enable us to inspect it ; and our object had been to see the Temple of Serapis, of
which a few relics yet remain in Puzzuoli.
The ancient baths here have been replaced by
modern ones, and this, added to the vicinity of

numerous cottages, has a bad effect. Three pillars are standing, and certain parts of the baths, but there is little of interest. Cicero's villa occupied an eminence near this temple, and the site may be seen from it. It is covered with orange groves, which also look down upon the fallen columns and dilapidated baths of Serapis. Returning to the sea-shore we beheld the remains of Caligula's Bridge, which it is said this emperor designed to carry over to Baiæ. It now extends but a little way, and is so broken as to resemble stepping-stones placed across a brook : the arches are completely gone. On the right is the town of Cumæ, celebrated for its vicinity to the Sybil's cave. The market-place of Puzzuoli has an ancient statue erected to the memory of M. Flavius. On our way back we met the Duke of Calabria and two ladies of the royal family, who had descended from their carriages and were walking in the dust of the public road ; a singular taste surely ! The duke returned our salutation with much politeness.

We dined on board the Cambrian, and, though the wind was contrary, beat out of the bay early on the following morning for Genoa, by order of the admiral, for the purpose of conveying Sir Manley Power to Malta. On Saturday and Sunday it blew heavily, and not a few of us suffered. On Tuesday it became calm, and a shark about six feet long was observed following the ship, accompanied by six or eight prettily marked fish, called *pilot-fish*. We endeavoured to hook him, but could not succeed, and he was at last shot by an officer of the ship, Lieut. Christie, an admirable marksman: the ball entered his neck, and appeared to have penetrated the heart; he rolled over, and, before a boat could be lowered, sunk to the bottom.

Wednesday, 1st Dec.——This day and yesterday the men were ordered to fire the main-deck guns at a mark, about one hundred and fifty yards distant. Several excellent shots were made. Still calm.

Thursday, 2d Dec.——A fine breeze, " fair as breeze may be," sprang up last night, and has continued all the day. Early this morning we passed Monte Christi, Pianoso, and the Isle of Elba on the right, with the high land of Corsica on the left. The sun, breaking with difficulty through a thick cloud, gilded the snowy tops of the mountains with a bright rosy tinge. About noon we passed Cape Corso, and expect to reach our destination to-night.

Friday, 3d Dec.——Early this morning we come in sight of " Genoa la Superbe," as it has been styled; and certainly the beauty of its situation may warrant the appellation. It is built at the foot of the Appennines, which tower majestically around it. To the East, as we entered the bay, the rising sun gilded the highest peaks of the mountains, which were then enveloped in snow; and on the West, the dark purple cope of the morning discovered to us the outline of another bay, of considerable extent. The scenery here appears as if the waves of the sea had risen " mountains high," and in that position had been struck like the Phæacian ship in the Odyssey, by the angry power of Neptune. The undulations are a remarkable object in the spectacle, and supply its greatest charm.

Genoa is situated in a kind of amphitheatre, and its suburbs extend for many miles along the sea-shore. The numbers of detached villas, seated on every eminence, seem like stragglers from the main flock, which repose in the sun-

shine on a lower and more distant point. The
mole, on which the light-house stands, has been
a work of some labour, and adds to the picturesque appearance of the bay. But the town
itself by no means corresponds with the ideas
which the approach to it inspires. The streets
are extremely narrow ; and, with the exception of one or two, most miserable. There are,
however, some magnificent palaces, although
not, in their present state, sufficient to justify
Madame de Staël's high-flown assertion, that
the main street (the Strada Nuova) seems built
for a " *congress of kings.*" Most of them have
been painted externally, but the paint is now
nearly effaced. Many of the noblest stair-
cases are dilapidated ; and the venders of fruits,
engravings, &c. occupy the lower parts of the
deserted mansion. The most striking thing in
Genoa, is the gay *mantilla* of the females,
although it is by no means general, the majority confining themselves to a simple white.
It is sufficiently worn, however, to give a peculiar and picturesque air to their appearance,
which is much increased by the regular and
handsome features exhibited beneath. This,
added to the cleanliness of their persons, gives

them a decided superiority over women of the like class at Naples. Yet the same disgusting smells prevail in the streets of Genoa; and *garlick*, in all its various degrees of rankness, breathes a sort of pestilence around them.

As the birth-place of Columbus and Andrea d'Auria, Genoa is entitled to respect; but it retains few monuments of antiquity, and those are of minor interest. Its paintings, indeed, which are numerous and rich, will long continue to attract the stranger; and the marble statues, which decorate some of its palaces and churches, are, no doubt, deserving every attention. But with few exceptions, I should describe Genoa, notwithstanding what has been said of its commercial importance, as one vast ruin. The principal palaces are uninhabited and desolate; and even the residence of the celebrated D'Auria is neglected and hastening rapidly to decay. His statue has not found a better fate : stones, " weeds, and ordure, rankle round the base."

The Ducal palace, (destroyed by fire in 1777, two years previous to the change of government,) a building of considerable extent, has been converted into public offices. It contains a magnificent saloon, where the Senate meet, ornamented with paintings in stucco, and marble pillars of the Corinthian order. A gallery for the convenience of spectators runs along the summit. They shew here the prow of a Roman ship, *said* to be the remains of one employed in the defence of Genoa against Mago, the Carthagenian general. The reader may believe or reject this story, as he thinks proper.

Amongst the other marvels of Genoa, there is an extraordinary cup, entitled *Sacro Catino*, which has been the subject of much discussion. It ought to be mentioned in an account of the Cathedral of St. Laurence; but, as it is doubtful whether I shall think it meet to gratify the reader in this case, although the church in question resembles a marble magpie, and has the unfortunate Saint, after whom it is named, broiling upon a gridiron above its gate, I shall proceed to extract from an authentic history whatever the Genoese have thought good to promulgate concerning it. And here, again, I submit the account to the pleasure of the reader.

" On conserve, dans la sacristie de cette

Métropolitaine, un monument des plus pré-
cieux que l'on connaisse ; c'est le vase d'Eme-
raude, connu *dans toute la Chretiénneté* sur
le nom de *Sacro Catino*, trouvé à la prise de
Césarée en la Palestine, faite par le vaillant
Guillaume *Embriaco* en 1101. Ce vase fut
choisi par les Gênois de preférence à tous les
biens de la ville. Le gouvernement Français
s'en empara en 1809, et il fut transporté à
Paris jusqu'à la paix de 1815, qui fut rendu
avec tous les objets d'arts enlevés pendant la
Revolution. Il est gardé soigneusement, et
on obtient difficilement la permission de le
voir. La grandeur de ce *Catino* est d'un pan
sept onces et demie, mesure de Gênes, sa cir-
conférence est de cinq pans moins un once ; il
est de forme exagone ayant deux anses, dont
une est polie et l'autre ebauchée. On pretend
que c'est dans ce vase que Notre Seigneur
mangea l'Agneau pascal avec ses disciples.
Les critiques les plus habiles ne sont pas d'ac-
cord sur cette pretention, quoiqu'il en soit, c'est
une pièce precieuse et fort ancienne, puisque l'on
va jusqu'à dire, qu'elle faisait partie des presens
que la *Reine de Saba offrit à Salomon et qui
étaient gardés dans les trésors du temple.*"

This venerable *Emerald* cup was carefully examined by the French savans, and ascertained, beyond doubt, to be composed of glass! But the remainder of its merits is, I suppose, yet under consideration. Could antiquaries prove it to have belonged to the queen of Sheba, they might probably trace up its origin still higher? Who knows but that Adam may have presented it to Methuselah; who might hand it to Noah. Noah might transmit it to Shem, Ham, or Japheth; and Shem, Ham, or Japheth, to some of their acquaintance. How the queen of Sheba came by it, may not be quite clear; but since she presented it to Solomon, there can be no dispute about her having possessed it. Harder matters than this have been got over; and the public may shortly expect to see a profound dissertation on the subject. I wish, with all my heart, that this point *was* satisfactorily determined; not only for the comfort of the Genoese, but for the honour of Solomon, and the queen of Sheba.

The Church of Notre Dame des Vignes, is one of the most ancient and distinguished. The nave is supported by sixteen columns of solid marble, and the ceiling beautifully painted by Paganetto. But then, that which renders it remarkable, is "*un tableau de la Sainte Vierge, trouvé miraculeusement en* 1603."

However, in despite of the surprising circumstance here recorded, the most beautiful structure in Genoa, in my opinion, is the Church of St. Mary de Carignan. It was built at the sole expence of the family of Saoli, in imitation, as it is said, of St. Peter's at Rome. But the similarity is denied by Mr. Eustace. One great merit of this building is the chaste and simple style of the decorations of its interior, contrasted with the vitiated taste of the rest of the Genoese churches. Four colossal statues by Puget are admirable; and especially one of St. Sebastian undergoing the tortures of martyrdom. The face is marked by an expression of the keenest agony; and the body seems actually to writhe in the bitterness of mortal suffering. Here are some fine pictures also by Piola, Carlo Maratti, Procaccini, and Guercino. From the gallery of the highest cupola, there is an extensive prospect of Genoa on the East; and on the opposite quarter, the eye enjoys a beautiful diversity of mountains

13

and valleys, country seats, and trelliced walks, covered with vines. To the right is the sea; over which fishing-boats skim with their felucca sails. Further on is a large bay; and to the left rise the mountains, crowned with fortified posts: here and there a church, with other picturesque appearances. On a fine day the Island of Corso can be distinguished from this point. Close by the church is the bridge of Carignan, which unites two hills. It is composed of seven arches, but has little to recommend it except its immense elevation. A street is below, and the tops of the loftiest houses, though many of them seven stories high, are seen far beneath it. At this time they were drying wheat, which was spread out in nicely arranged portions upon the pavement of the bridge.

The Hon. Captain Spenser, of the Naiad, sailed a few days before our arrival at Genoa. He brought the Sardinian court information of a pacific arrangement having been made with the Algerine powers, in place of an expected war. It seems his most gracious majesty was so delighted with the intelligence, that he ordered on board, as a present to the

15

English frigate, *a calf and a basket of vegetables.* Captain Spenser directed the consul
to pay for them, supposing, perhaps, that such
unbounded liberality might reduce too materially the state's revenue !—A consideration
highly laudable, and which, I trust, his majesty
will duly estimate.

Tuesday, 7th Dec.—On Monday evening
I was present at the representation of one
of Goldoni's comedies, at the theatre San
Augustino : I thought the acting excellent.
This evening the puppets, at one of the minor
theatres, afforded me considerable diversion.
The plot, as far as I could understand it, represented a nun, who had transgressed her
vows. She is struck with remorse, and consumes her days in "penitence and prayer."
The devil, enraged at the loss of a proselyte,
endeavours to draw her back into error, but is
put to flight by a furious speech of her con-
fessor, who enters during the struggle. The
last scene discovers the penitent on her death-
bed, and the monk exhorting her to be of
good cheer. The whole of this was admirable.
The faint melancholy tones of the expiring
sinner, her mental and corporeal exhaustion,

were excellently well acted. The puppet, at intervals, elevated the hands and the head, so as to give great effect to what was going on. Perhaps an exception might be taken to the colour of the cheeks; they were certainly too rubious; yet the spectator might indeed have concluded, that her repentance was of a most *cordial* nature. But, in short, infinitely more pathos was manifested than I should have thought it possible to represent by mechanism. An interlude followed, representing harlequin and his wife dancing to the music of three grotesque figures. This ended in a battle-royal, and so, *exeunt omnes.* The concluding part of the performance was very long and very stupid. It consisted in a succession of scenes without meaning, save that it appeared a most unhappy effort to dramatize certain passages of Ariosto. There were griffins and hypogriffins, Archimagos and Bradamantes, " tag-rag and bob-tail three or four scores." I employed the whole of this day in running over certain palaces; the Cambrian having been detained by contrary winds. It was, indeed, the Captain's intention to sail on the very day of our arrival, provided Sir Manley and Lady Power could so arrange it. But his sister-in-law, a daughter of Lieutenant-General Cockburn, happening to be then in Genoa, Sunday was fixed for our departure. Unfavourable weather has since kept us in harbour.

I wish to observe, that in the desultory observations I have made relating to the capital of Liguria, I have been led by a desire to avoid as much as possible the common track of other travellers; not only because of the small degree of interest which it appears to me this place is capable of exciting; but because it would only be a wearisome repetition of what others have said. I have, therefore, omitted many things which might, perhaps, have been detailed in a journal, as well in this as at other places which we have visited. I have no intention to present a guide-book to the public. Whatever strikes me, I shall commit to paper; embodying such reflections as the occasion may suggest, without much regard to systematic arrangement. Details of pictures, and statues, and palaces, are, at best, but a mawkish kind of reading:—people rarely agree about these things, or rise much better or wiser from the perusal. And it would be impossible to con-

vey, even to an *amateur*, any considerable
portion of that pleasure which an inspection
of the originals may have produced. But the
majority of mankind are not amateurs; and,
of those who call themselves such, how many
are governed by affectation, by fashion,—by
any thing but a real taste. A book, therefore,
which abounds much in these matters, may
not be a bad book; but the chances are greatly
in favour of its being thought so. In reality,
these are subjects which should be seen,—not
read of; examined in person,—not judged of
at second-hand. As a taste for them cannot
be acquired by reading, so neither by reading
can a matured taste find a solid gratification.
It is the feast of the Barmecide; subtile, un-
substantial fare; a vapour exhaled by the ap-
petite, and lost in the warmth of its embrace.
Descriptions of natural objects, on the other
hand, I shall omit no opportunity of giving.
Here the scene lives—breathes: art has not
contaminated its beauty, nor diminished the
brilliancy of its character. Instead of a feeble
copy, the eye dwells upon a glowing original;
and the impression, which it carries to the
feelings, has a vividness and a fidelity of re-

flection which not unfrequently penetrates to the heart of the reader. It may be consecrated by the past glory of man, or it may exist only in its own; but in either case it speaks with all the luxury of sentiment, and all the loveliness of truth.

Wednesday, 8th Dec.——Early this morning a gun was fired from the ship as a signal for departure. About nine o'clock Major General Sir Manley Power and his family came on board, and the Cambrian set sail immediately after.

The swell has been considerable to-day, though it is now perfectly calm.

Friday, 10th Dec.——This morning we passed the Islands of Gorgona and Capriara, blowing pretty freshly. Elba and Monte Christi were on our lee-bow about noon.

Monday, 13th Dec.——It blew exceedingly hard all yesterday night, but the wind was fair; they term it a *Grecario*, it is the north-east, and by seven this morning brought us to Malta. The waves ran high, and dashed beautifully against the rocks as we entered the harbour of Valetta.

In the evening was the first public ball of

this season.   The assembly room, once the residence of a knight of Malta, is of magnificent
dimensions, as indeed most of their houses
were.   It possesses a property in which others
are deficient, that of having a boarded floor,
but the value of this is very greatly diminished
by the customary flooring of stone beneath.
However, as there is not another thing of the
kind in the island, it must be considered a
great acquisition.   I had the pleasure to meet
again Captain (now Major) and Mrs. Fox at
this ball, who, it seems, have fixed their residence at La Floriana, about a mile distant from
the capital.   Mrs. Fox is looking remarkably
well, and appears highly satisfied with her new
abode : this pleases me, for very few have the
power of creating and securing esteem more
effectually than Mrs. Charles Fox.   The truly
feminine softness of her manner, aided by the
kindness and goodness of her heart, possesses
an almost irresistible attraction, and leaves her
friends doubtful whether she should be prized
more for the gentleness of disposition which
prompts, or for the natural delicacy of character
which envelopes and embalms her every action.
For many a really kind feeling has been ren-

dered nugatory by the method which some
people adopt in discovering it; and many a
good deed has become inefficient and revolting, merely from the want of a delicate consideration, a generous *expression* as well as a
generous thought. It is the failure in this
which makes obligations so odious, and ingrati-
tude so common. Motives are apt to be mistaken, not less when favours are conferred than
when they are denied; and I have frequently
known more pain communicated by the first
than by the second: all this arises purely from
manner, and therefore I feel justified in ap-
plauding, and even in joining it (where they
both equally exist) with the native feeling
which precedes and probably generates it. I
would almost lay it down as an axiom, that
a benevolent feeling will necessarily produce
benevolent expression, whatever may be the
harshness of feature, or general want of polish,
in the individual who experiences it; and that
whenever it is otherwise all is not as it should
be. There is a material defect somewhere;
and I am also persuaded that this expression,
when not the result of its proper feeling, can
never be assumed: imitation and artifice may

do much, but they cannot vary with circumstances so minute as are required here; they
cannot copy what they neither see nor understand; a general outline may in some cases be
caught up, but it will scarcely deceive the most
inexperienced. It is the genuine child of sympathy, the natural consequence of an understanding head and a feeling heart, and without
these the master-chord of another's bosom will
never respond.

Major Fox on this occasion introduced me
to the Rev. Mr. Cleugh, the government chaplain. I think him a valuable acquaintance.

Tuesday, 14*th Dec.*—I breakfasted with Mr.
Cleugh, and afterwards rode with him to St.
Antonio, a country seat of the Marquis of
Hastings. The prospect is very peculiar; it
resembles a desolate waste with a few straggling patches of verdure in certain fortunate
situations; yet even these the dryness of the
soil, which is chiefly formed of the pounded
rock and perchance some minute particles of
compost, together with the warmth of the atmosphere, render so parched that a bright spot
of green is seldom visible. In some places it
is impossible for a calèche to travel; and one

is surprized that even the sure-footed ponies, so common in this country, can maintain their ground. As we passed along, a number of Maltese were fishing in an angle of the harbour for shrimps, or rather *prawns*, which alone are caught here. Their method is, to drop small nets attached to a hoop into the water, with baits fastened to the meshes; a cork, connected with the net, floats above, and this apparatus is deposited at intervals along the shore. They pass from one to another, and examine their contents by means of a kind of wooden fork with two prongs, which catches hold of the float and raises the net. Half a dozen prawns at a time is as much as they catch; but their patience, or as others term it, their indolence, is invincible. In returning we passed an aqueduct of some importance, which communicates with La Valetta ;—this work was effected by the knights of Malta : the harbours form beautiful objects from a great variety of points, dividing one town from another on each side of the capitol : thus it may be called a mountain Venice, or as Lord Byron has said of the latter, with less propriety perhaps,

" She looks a sea Cybele, fresh from ocean,
    Rising with her tiara of proud towers
  At airy distance, with majestic motion,
    A ruler of the waters and their powers :"

for the town is built upon a rock of considerable magnitude, and a small Grecian temple,
erected to the memory of Sir Alexander Ball,
crowns the summit of the point which first
catches the eye on entering the harbour of
Valetta. Besides which, the surrounding fortifications, which wind in every possible diversity
of form, might give an additional impulse to
an imaginative mind :——to such I leave the
matter.

Wednesday, 15th Dec.——This day was employed in rambling up and down Valetta in
pursuit of old books : many a dusty volume
did I turn over, and many a fat worm trembled
in its narrow confines as I adventured forth. I
found little, however, of moment ; though from
the various revolutions which Malta has seen,
and the probable ransacking of the monastery,
libraries, &c. some curious volumes might have
been looked for ; but I apprehend that there
have been some diligent investigators before
me. Amongst others, I obtained " Traité de

l'Administration des'Bois de l'Ordre de Malte, dependans de ses Grands-Prieurés, Bailliages et Commanderies dans le Royaume de France." Printed at Paris in 4to. 1757, " avec approbation et permission." This book is a presentation copy from the author to the Grand Master Emanuel Pinto, the last Superior, as he is called, of the order. In courage and ability he equalled at least, if he did not surpass, the most celebrated of his predecessors; and the weakness and inanity of the few who succeeded him place them out of all competition. The book in question is handsomely bound in Russia, with the arms of the grand master stamped and gilded on the back : it seems to have been published anonymously, but this being a presentation copy the author's name is subscribed in manuscript at the close of the Epistle Dedicatory. It appertains to the conservation of the woods belonging to the order, with forms of various instruments relating thereto. Another volume, a thin quarto, printed at Lyons in 1755, is entitled " Modele pour Servir à la Reception de Messieurs les Chevaliers de Malte." The author, M. Le Chevalier de Laube de Bron, Commendeur de Tortebesse, informs us in the preface, that he was desired by the venerable Tongue of Auvergne to undertake this work; but that for a long time a prudent mistrust of his own powers induced him to decline it; at last " il s'est cru obligé de se prêter aux volontés du corps." This work, as well as the other, is valuable from having been published under the control of the order.

In a small quarto volume of tracts appears a curious Latin speech of Pope Clement XIV. to the Secret Consistory; an academical exercise; a sermon, preached in the Maltese Cathedral on the shipwreck of St. Paul, " primario tutelare dell' isole di Malta, e Gozzo," by P. Gio. Maria Regnaud, a Jesuit, in 1749; with a second, on the Apostle's conversion. There is also a theological disputation; but the greatest curiosity in the volume is a host of fulsome panegyrics, alternately in Italian and Latin, by a Maltese poet, ycleped Damiro Carisio. The subject is the fifth anniversary of the Grand Mastership of Emanuel de Rohan. It is printed in Malta 1780, and dedicated to " his most serene highness." The reader shall be made happy with a specimen of the larger effusions. The following opens the Latin poem.

" Quo vehor ô Vates? procul ô procul este profani :
Limina jamque datum Phœbeæ scandere sedis
Est mihi, et Aonidum latices haurire perennes.
Eja, age, rumpe moras, Dea candida, rumpe, celerque
Aoniam mentem Vati mihi conde canenti :
Tuque prior præsens claro de sanguine cretus
Huc ades, ô PRINCEPS, nostrisque allabere cœptis.
Fallor ego? en subito cœlestis fulgor ab axe
Mortales hebetat visus, mentemque recursat
Irradians, crebra tellus sub luce refulsit :
Quales ingeminant abruptis nubibus ignes,
Horrida cum cœlo eripuit mortalibus ægris
Tempestas sine morâ diem, lucemque fugavit ;
Hinc exaudiri magnum per inane fragores.
Aligerum glomerata phalanx audita sonantes
Pulsare et cytheras, numerosque intendere nervis ;
Candida cœruleas fluitant vexilla per auras
Clara micanti auro, positisque ex ordine gemmis :
Gloria devehitur curru connixa nitenti
Visa Dea incessu rosea cervice refulgens,
Æthereumque levis summum perlabitur axem :
Dulcia cœlesti testatur gaudia plausu"—

But can the most gentle reader apprehend a
reason for all this exquisite hubbub? Surely

" Quòd ROHAN EMANUEL, sceptris qui temperat urbem,
Cui studuit cœlum, felix jam conficit annum
Imperii quintum, protendens nomen in ævum!"

Thursday, 16*th Dec.*—I had made an ap-

pointment with **Mr. Cleugh** to ride this morning to a singular valley, denominated (κατ'
ἐξοχὴν, I imagine,) the *strong valley*. It is very
curious in its way, and resembles the exhausted
bed of a river. The soil, as we rode along,
barely covered the rock ; and the scanty vege-
tation seemed like the violent struggle of nature
and necessity for conquest.

> " Truly to speak, sir, and, with no addition,
>   To pay five ducats, five, I would not farm it."

· The *carūbba*, which is the only tree in Malta
that appears to flourish, affords the chief part of
the subsistence of the islanders. It yields a kind
of bean which is also given to cattle; and indeed the food of their masters is seldom other,
or better. This fruit, with a little fish, satisfies
them ; but the latter is scarce. This easiness
of obtaining a bare existence, if it have not
rendered them indolent, has probably contributed to make them appear so. Being content
with little, and the produce which their country
supplies being attainable by creating, not till-
ing, a soil; by communicating verdure to the
rock, not by directing or assisting a natural
fertility ; no wonder if they should look with

despair upon a labour so unpromising, and
turn with disgust from hardships for which they
can expect so slight a remuneration.   Yet
wherever industry would be available, they appear readily to have exercised it.   The valley,
of which I speak, bears ample testimony to
this truth.   The smallest space, whether upon
the summit or upon the sides of the rock, has
had the stone broken and cultivated; walls are
raised for inclosures; and steps, constructed
with much neatness and skill, afford a passage
upward from one field or compartment to another.   These places are open to every incle-
mency of the weather; and though its mutations are rare, yet in the rainy season, the
water rushes down with tremendous force, and,
in a single night, sweeps away the whole expected harvest of the husbandman.   But his
perseverance is greater than his loss; he re-
sumes his laborious occupation beneath a burning sun, and gathers, at last, the very limited
recompence which nature's parsimony admits.
The excessive idleness of the Maltese has been
too much and too invidiously dwelt upon. Instances to the contrary there are of course;
but the native character appears to me dis-

posed to activity. Subjugated as they have
been, and rendered the tool of every faction,
ecclesiastical as well as civil, can we be surprised that they should then shun the labour of
which they were not permitted to eat the fruit;
and, becoming habituated to idleness, can we
imagine that they should cast off long-existing
evils at the beck of a new government; or,
that years should not elapse before they could
assume a more energetic character, and a
manlier tone of mind? It has been confessed
to me, that they are skilful workmen, and good
soldiers, (there is a corps in the pay of the
government,) and I see continual proofs of a
persevering industry, from which those who
hold them cheap would turn away in despair,
yet I hear every where the cant of their lazi-
ness; whereas a strenuous effort to improve
and amend them would better become the
station and the heart of the prejudiced de-
claimer. Civilization will never go forward as
it ought, if such feelings continue to dwell
in the minds of those who are alone able
to give this people effectual assistance; and
if so much narrow calculation, as commonly
occupies the thoughts of those in whose way

they are thrown, should continue to prevail, it will be vain to look for that reciprocity of spirit and sentiment, which can alone indissolubly unite two remote and differing people.

The evening of this day was occupied by a pleasant dance at Major Fox's.

Friday, 17*th Dec.*—I resumed my search after books, and discovered one or two upon which I set some value. For instance, a very beautiful manuscript, entitled, " Regles et Maximes des Statuts de l'Ordre de Malta. Pour Messire Anthoine de Sade Eyguières Commendeur d'Espalion en 1715." This work being unpublished, and containing a full account of all the regulations touching the knights of Malta, is extremely interesting. And the authenticity of its details is obvious, from its having been drawn up under the direction and for the use of a commander of the order. It is a tolerably thick quarto, comprising 423 closely-written pages, together with a copious index. It seems to have been three years in progress, if we may trust the first page of the MS. " A Malte le premier jour du mois de Janvier de l'année 1712." There is, indeed,

15

much curious matter in it.   As for instance, " *De la table du pillier.*"

" First,—Two soups, without garnish; two dishes of boiled veal, weighing ten pounds and a half each.

" Two dishes of roasted mutton, weighing ten pounds each; the dish *du regale* of nine singing birds, when the grand commander eats there, besides four roasted pigeons.

" *Item*,—Two dishes of fricassee; two plates of radishes, figs, or melons, according to the season; two dishes of boiled mutton for the valets of the ancients, who eat in the pillary, *(au pillier;)* seven grains a day to each of the ancients for two other dishes of fricassee, that they may serve three grains in the morning and four grains at night; six dishes of desert according to the season."

And then of those who eat at the *Auberge*, it seems, that they were not to spill their wine upon the ground " on pain of the *seton*, (' sur peine de la settane';)" nor to carry out of it any kind of provision on the same singular penalty.   Also, whoever complains " *mal-a-propos*," as the MS. phrases it, of what is

13

given at the Auberge, " pour la premiere fois la *settane* et seconde aussy."

Whoever beats the valets of the Pillary, but without shedding blood, was, for the first offence, to be condemned to a *quarantine*,—a fast of forty days; for the second, six months' fast in the day time; for the third, he lost two years of seniority. Nobody was to enter the kitchen against the will and pleasure of the " *maistre de sale,*" on penalty of the seton for the first and second offence, the quarantine for the third.

" The ancients of France, Italy, Spain, and Germany, eat with the grand master on feast days. They did not wash their hands at the conclusion of the repast as the others did; but went from the table, and placed themselves behind the chair of the grand master, who ought to oblige them to cover." [Faire couvrer —perhaps *the table.*]

" When the pillar of England goes to court, the grand master ought to salute him with the hat, and to make him cover when he goes to see him dine. He eats with the grand master when he goes to see him in the country."— *Et cætera.*

Saturday, 18*th Dec.*—I was present, by ac-
cident, at a Catholic ordination of priests, in
the cathedral church of St. John.   The bishop
is a corpulent creature, and remarkable, if report speak truly, more for being a *bon vivant*,
and an *amoureux*, than for devotion.   Some
disgraceful stories are related of him.   The
most striking point of the ordination in question, was this : the cope of the candidate was
rolled to the top of his back, and after the
laying on of hands, was unrolled by the bishop,
who flung it behind the kneeling person.   He
wore a pasteboard mitre, embossed and gilt,
to which two broad strings were appended.
The crowd consisted chiefly of women and
children.

Sunday, 19*th Dec.*—I preached at the chapel of the palace, and dined with the Reverend
John T. H. Le Mesurier, chaplain to the forces.
I heard a curious story of the attachment of
an old Maltese to his goat.   He was upwards
of eighty years of age, and lived entirely apart
from all society.   Without family, and almost
without friends, his goat had been a cherished
object from its birth ; and he had so accustomed
himself to its society, that he seemed not to

feel the want or the wish for any other. It happened, that some inconstancy on the part of the goat led it to ramble from the humble residence of its aged friend, and it found its way to the house of the gentleman where I heard the story. The old Maltese fell into the greatest tribulation; he sought for it all over Floriana, and, for a time, without success. At last he discovered where the truant had retired; thither he went, and had no sooner beheld it than he burst into a flood of tears. He embraced and kissed it, with every demonstration of extreme joy, and nothing would prevail upon him to quit the sight of it for a single moment. The goat too shewed considerable signs of repentance, and returned joyfully to her old abode. I remembered the story of the captive who cultivated an intimacy with a spider; the agony ascribed to him when it fell by the wanton brutality of his keeper; and it appeared to turn upon the same desolateness of feeling, the same necessity for some object on which to fix the social affections. One would have thought, that eighty years had dried up the fount of sensibility, and that the humble condition of his life would have converted all such emotions into a cureless apathy. Conceive an old sallow-complexioned creature, with grey dirty hair, exhaling garlick, and girded with threadbare rags; and then imagine him giving vent to the feelings of a full heart, while he clasped his recovered goat with even more than youthful enthusiasm! Such a picture is but rarely to be met with.

Monday, 20th Dec.—The public library of Malta, where I spent the greater part of this morning, is a good building, and of ample size. The books are not classed with much judgment, and indeed have, until the appointment of the present obliging librarian, the Abbe Bellanti, been greatly neglected, or rather injured. For it seems the French helped themselves to the best portion, and left the remainder in a state of ruinous disorder. A fine large-paper copy of Walton's Polyglott has been preserved here, with an Arabic or Maltese Bible, ornamented with beautiful engravings.

We have experienced the greatest civility from all quarters, save in my own person, and tremble thou unhappy varlet! save from the *over-looker* of the Botanic Garden at Floriana. Rightly have I named him; while I loitered within his precincts, this wicked gardener did *overlook* me, and locked me up to study botany, and watch the motions of a brace of becaficas which were hopping unconcernedly from spray to spray. I waited patiently, nay, with very singular patience, till I could wait no longer! And then I reared a huge ladder, drew it with great difficulty and some danger over a high wall, and descended, muttering no light anathema upon the abominable gardener. Verily,

" My indignation boileth like a pot,
An over-heated pot, still, still it boileth ;
It boileth, and it bubbleth with disdain."

CHAPTER IV.

TUESDAY, 21st *Dec.*—Set sail from Malta, and ran, with a fair wind, up the *arches,* as the Archipelago is termed by seamen; a term which future ages will pore over and elucidate by many a sagacious commentary.

Thursday, 23d *Dec.*—Stood off Cerigo,— the ancient Cythera, this morning. The fortress is in possession of an English garrison. A boat was sent on shore with letters, while the Cambrian lay to for her return. The commanding officer, unadvisedly as it would seem, came back in the boat, by which circumstance we were detained during the whole day.

Friday, 24th *Dec.*—Off Milo, where we took in a pilot. This town is situated upon a rock, at the foot of which is a fine bay, containing numerous inlets of great beauty. Several curious rocks rise up at the entrance;

of these Anti-milo is considered the largest. A barren rock to the left is pointed out as the residence of one Dromede, a school-master, who went thither with his scholars for the sake of retirement. The matter is not worth much notice. At Milo I distributed four modern Greek Testaments, and four Italian; being part of a quantity sent to Captain Hamilton, for that purpose, by the Bible Society *. The captain desired me to undertake the distribution.

Mr. Wilson, a missionary, sent out, as I understand, by a sect of the Methodists, obligingly presented me with a copy of Bunyan's Pilgrim's Progress, which he had translated into Romaic, and superintended the printing of in Malta. This gentleman appears to me the most liberal of the sect I have met with, and to conduct himself in the pursuit of his object with more discretion than his brethren have had the credit of observing. He spoke of several elementary books for children, in which his industry and zeal had prompted him to engage; and of a certain philological performance relative to the Greek tongue, with some

* They were afterwards returned to me.

other matters which I forget. The account
which he gave of the Greeks, after an acquaintance of five years, is much more favourable than I could even have hoped ; well as I
wish their cause, and think of the result. Their
clergy received most of his censure, but that
was of a qualified kind. On the whole, though
he acknowledged that the Greeks had many
and great vices, yet he was firmly persuaded
of the exaggeration and malice with which
their actions had been misrepresented and
traduced.

At Spetzia we landed Mr. Wilson and his
cargo of tracts, Bibles, and Prayer-books : a
Greek schooner of war was cruizing up and
down the offing, and the beach was crowded
with spectators. It is said, that 179 Turkish
sail of the line are wasting away their time in
the harbours of Candia.

Late this evening we anchored off Napoli di
Romania, the ancient Nauplia.

Saturday, 25th Dec. CHRISTMAS-DAY.—
After performing divine service on board the
Cambrian, I hastened to make what use I could
of the little time allowed, to inspect Napoli di
Romania. This town is situated at the foot of

a high rock, surmounted by a fortress called
the Palamedes. I saw it first at sun-rise, from
the sea. Landing on the quay, we were instantly in the midst of a crowd of Greeks;
and I cannot describe the elation of spirit
which I experienced on first touching with
my foot this celebrated soil. It matters
little with how many sapient smiles feelings of
such a nature may be greeted; nor with how
much contumely phlegmatic minds may dwell
upon the warm and stirring emotions which
arise at the contemplation of a land of departed
greatness, and reviving freedom. I do not
grudge them their laugh, provided they are
sure that they understand the occasion of it;
and if, while they look on the fading monuments of the old world, the relics, as it were,
of antediluvian majesty, they can stand with
cold and self-sufficient apathy, like the bird of
Pallas over the ruins of her temple; or mark
the advance of freedom with the dull calculating eye of politicians rather than of men, I
shall be well satisfied to go my way in solitude.
I seek not their communion; they may be
wiser, but not happier; they may see more
acutely, but they see not half so joyously:

11

and the mind being thus rigid and harsh,
what impression shall there be made upon the
heart? They want sympathy with suffering,
and admiration for glory: they can behold
" decay's effacing fingers" busy without a
sigh, and hear the blast of desolation sweep
along the broken wrecks of antiquity with the
most frigid indifference! Then what are they to
me, or I to them? They will not appreciate, for
they cannot comprehend, the feeling with which
I stood upon an eminence beyond the citadel
of the Palamedes; below, the town of Napoli
with its white houses and churches; the bay,
with the little fort of St. Theodore in the midst,
(now converted into a prison, to which at that
very moment Giovanni Notara, son of one of
the principal rebels confederated with Colocotroni, was led,) Argos, with its acropolis shining
in the sun; the flat marshy ground extending
like an amphitheatre from thence to Napoli;
the Lacædemonian mountains rising in double
volumes in front, and those beyond Argos
capped with snow; the Cambrian riding in
the bay,—for,

 " A stately-builded ship, well rigg'd, and tall,
  The ocean maketh more majestical;"

with numberless little fishing-boats skimming
along the water; and more immediately beneath, the Greeks, in their picturesque costumes, galloping here and there upon spirited
ponies over the rough paths of the declivity;
with sheep and goats browsing upon the sides
of the rocks, and women in the distance washing their linen at a public well: there an over-
thrown Turkish cemetery, where all was trebly
desolate; a farm-house, and what appeared a
small fortress, a little beyond it on a lofty
eminence:—all these were to me objects of an
intense and overwhelming interest.

The streets of Napoli are extremely narrow,
and they were, at this time, filled with Greeks.
It was the market-day, and numbers of the
peasantry had come from Argos, and the adjoining country, to dispose of their produce.
The shops were full of wares, and, amongst
other things, guns, pistols, and sabres were
exposed to sale. They were, for the most
part, fine healthy-looking men, and prepossessed me considerably in their favour. But
they seem to carry their arms awkwardly; and
it is not to be wondered at, when we remember that they consist of a ponderous brace

13

of pistols, a sabre, ataghan or dagger, with a long gun in addition ; in short, each of them, as Churchill pleasantly observes * on another occasion,——

> " Seemed to be
> A little moving *armoury*."

The pistols are often very richly chased, and their skin capotes, or cloaks, turbaned heads, (for many of them adopt the Turkish costume) and gay sashes and garters give a picturesque and pleasing air to their appearance.   I felt that I was in a strange land more forcibly than ever I had done before ; all was new and exciting. Passing through the gates of the city, having the fortress of the Palamedes on the right, we noticed upwards of twenty soldiers on guard. The feeling produced by regarding our own regularly organized troops in contrast with the grotesque body before us was very striking ; yet they had a martial cast of countenance, and could not, with all our prejudices in favour of a more advanced state of civilization, be held contemptible.   A little beyond the town

* *The Ghost.*

is the remains of the Turkish cemetery before alluded to : the walls are thrown down, the tombs destroyed, and the stone turbans usually placed above a Mussulman's sepulchre are scattered in every direction——here lay a broken Turkish inscription, there the *Athanaton* (a tree of considerable size) torn up by the roots, with the aloe still flourishing. Amongst the ruins was a Greek woman collecting herbs, which grew with mournful fecundity. Up the ascent of the rocks appeared a number of caves, which I took to be the shelter of goats or sheep, but they proved to be the abodes of human beings : in one a kettle boiled over a charcoal fire ; a small quantity of woollen cloth was rolled up in a corner, which, with an earthen dish, completed the arrangement. It was unoccupied, but the tenant, I presume, was tending the flock at no great distance. I noticed a good deal of squills in these parts.

On returning I was more than ever struck with the height and curious appearance of the rock which forms the basis of the citadel. It is nearly perpendicular, and jagged in an extraordinary manner ; it seemed as if thus left by the *pickaxes* of the Cyclops, who are said

to have been marvellously busy in this neighbourhood ; as if the hands of giants had divided the mountain, and worked it into an
everlasting monument, while a race of pigmies
had succeeded to their habitations, and endeavoured, with feeble and abortive efforts, to
emulate their labours.

After a walk of two or three hours it was
necessary to return to the ship.   The yawl had
already gone, and I found some difficulty in
engaging a boat to carry me out, for the wind
had risen, and there was considerable swell.
Former travellers complain of the extortion of
the Greeks : what they might have been I
know not, and I have as yet had small opportunity to ascertain what they are at present ;
but I was told a horse might be had at Napoli
to convey me to Argos, (a distance of twelve
miles) for a quarter of a dollar ; and for a like
sum, a large boat and two men brought me to
the ship.   It was necessary to make four tacks,
the spray dashed over us every minute, and
the man at the helm must have been wet
through.

I heard on board the ship, from some of the
passengers, who, not having engagements, were

enabled to get round to Argos, that a rebel, the son of Notara, had, as I before hinted, been seized and led a prisoner to the fortress of St. Theodore. He was described to me as a fine-looking man, and the importance of the prize may be estimated by the number of men who composed his guard : these amounted nearly to a hundred—a motley company, who would fain have ridden along in some order but for their ignorance of what the word signified. They had a band, and amongst the instruments was a sort of guitar with two strings. I should like to have seen this—was it the remains of the ancient KIΘAPA ? Whilst we were at dinner the principal senator of Napoli came on board to pay his respects to the captain. A papas, or Greek priest, accompanied by another of the authorities was with him. I offered the papas a number of Romaic and Italian Testaments; on examination he found that he possessed many more copies than he knew how to dispose of. I hope I am not unjust, but this fact clearly proves to me the little judgment with which the " *Bible Society*" distribute their volumes. The books, which this person had the charge of, were lying uselessly in his coffers;

exposed, in all human probability, to inevitable decay : and yet, every month immense pack-ages are forced into the country——what be-comes of them we may partly conjecture by the present instance.

Sunday, 26th Dec.——Early this morning we left the Gulf of Napoli.   It rained heavily, but, during a cessation, the scenery displayed a singularly beautiful diversity ; the mountains, forming part of the chain upon which the ci-tadel is built, were enveloped in thick mist ; the sides of the rocks upon our left were co-vered with green foliage, except upon the verge of the water, which presented a long white line intermingled with red tinges.   Over the pro-jecting promontory which terminated these rocks, a rainbow was finely suspended, while the opposite coast of mountains exhibited an intense blue, which reached along the whole line like a lowering thunder-cloud.   As we were advancing a solitary sun-beam broke through the density of the atmosphere, and these dark appearances assumed, in detached parts, an auburn tint——the tint of an autumn leaf.   The summits were crowned with fleecy clouds, and in the offing a little bark, with its light red sails expanded to the breeze, bore rapidly away.—Such was the prospect on leaving Napoli di Romania.

It continued to rain the greater part of the day:—about dusk we anchored off Spetzia.

Monday, 27th Dec.—Just as we were heaving the anchor a messenger came on board from Mr. Wilson, the missionary, with a letter for Captain Hamilton. It seems a Maltese brig had been chartered for five months by the Pacha of Egypt; after which he compelled the captain to convey a lading of Arabian horses to Candia, for the use of that government: on their way they were boarded by a Greek schooner, and the fact of their conveying property for the Turks being considered a breach of neutrality, they were taken and carried into Spetzia, where they now remain. The Turks threatened, according to the account of her captain, to cut his throat if he did not assent to their wishes;—but as yet we have heard but one side of the story. Of course, Captain Hamilton refused to interfere. It is pleasant to learn that our government has determined to grant the Greeks all the customary rights and privileges which are due from a neutral nation

to a belligerent power.   This is the first step
towards acknowledging their independence.

Tuesday Morning, 28th Dec.—We came
in sight of Cape Collonna, or Sunium, the scene
of Falconer's Shipwreck : it is more celebrated
for the Temple of Minerva Sunias, which stood
upon its summit.   The remains of this once
magnificent structure present a fine object from
the sea ; thence it appears entire, the front
pillars concealing the desolation which has
taken place.   The wind, called a Levanter,
blowing violently against us, it was thought
proper to come to an anchor in Porto Mandri,
the ancient Pantomatrio according to Sir
William Gell *, but this the increased force of
the gale rendered impracticable : we therefore
put about, and dropped anchor within two or
three miles from the Cape, in Porto Caracca.

A little after one o'clock we got on shore,
and walked with our guns by a circuitous
route to the temple.   The country is extremely
mountainous and barren, but dwarf cypresses
and myrtle, the mastick-tree and Velania oak
flourish both in the vallies and on the summits

---

* According to Dr. Sibthorpe, *Thoricus.*   See Walpole's Travels, 4to. p. 34.

of the hills. Game we found very scarce. On ascending Cape Sunium there is a fine prospect of the sea, over which the promontory beetles, and of five or six islands spread within the compass of the eye along this part of the Archipelago. The ruins of the temple itself are well worth inspection, but the wanton mischief to which it is continually exposed will leave little gratification to the future traveller. Dr. Clarke and Sir William Gell mention fifteen columns standing, there are now but fourteen, nine on the south-east side, looking upon the sea, three on the north, and two on the north-west. The cornice has been most grossly disfigured.

" BELLONA AUSTRIACA, 1824," in large letters of black paint, which may be seen at the distance of some miles, will remain an indelible stigma upon the whole Vandal crew of that Austrian vessel. Amongst the thousands of names which bedaub these columns, the one most conspicuous is that of " C. THURTELL, R. N." Lord Byron and Tweddel are also handed to immortality through the medium of the suffering column, but I am quite persuaded that his lordship had better taste

and better feeling than to employ himself in
such senseless mutilation; nor can I believe
less of Tweddel. Whoever may have been
the instrument, they stand a record of the most
egregious folly ; it is not only blameable in the
act itself, but it affords an ill and dangerous
example to the mass of travellers whom fate
and their own mischance send from their mother's apron-strings. A name cut upon the
stone leads by some inexplicable " tortuosity
of mind" to the cutting of another, and, if possible, a *larger*. Man scorns to be outdone ;
and the vast number of those who are thus
emulous must prove fatal to antiquity : if they
do not weaken the column, and hasten its entire destruction, which they certainly do, they
draw away the mind from the contemplation
of other times to anathematize the folly of our
own. The unseemly figures which are amassed
before the eye inspire very opposite feelings
to those which it is the tendency of such monuments to excite ; and one might as well, indeed infinitely better, so far as it affects the
heart or the understanding, look upon an ancient marble enveloped in modern cement, as
observe a beautiful Doric column covered with

names, of which a great portion are little honour to their owners, and cannot be more so to
the column itself. This is a real evil, and it
calls for public condemnation. With what intention do people scribble their ill-omened appellations upon the venerable relics of past
ages? Purely, as far as I can see, for the ridiculous fancy that they may be " syllabled" by
persons who never heard of them, and who do
not care one straw whether they ever hear of
them or not! Yet this exquisitely childish vanity effects more than Time in the ruin of antiquity, and prompts weak and inconsiderate
men to waste, with stupid indifference, monuments which nothing can repair. Let me say
it ; the breath that encircled the column——the
incense which floated around it, when in all
the pomp and plenitude of heathen magnificence, is chipped away by these unfeeling pre-
tenders to *vertu !*

" Ἑκὰς, ἱκάς ἐστε βεβήλοι !"

I found amid the ruins of the old town, a
little lower on the declivity, two handles of
terra-cotta vessels, " those indestructible and

infallible testimonies of places resorted to by the *Ancient Greeks* *." Dr. Clarke found no remains of this town, but to me they were very perceptible, extending a considerable distance down the hill ; and Chandler's opinion on this point seems quite borne out by facts. A signet ring of silver, found during Lord Strangford's excavations in the Acropolis of Athens when the Cambrian was last in the Archipelago, was presented to me this evening by Mr. Richmond Easto, the worthy and intelligent master of the frigate, himself the happy discoverer. The following is its figure,

and the inscription, which I have not as yet been able to decypher, runs thus when impressed upon wax.

* Clarke's Travels, Vol. VI.

All that I can make of the legend at present is
ΓΕΘΧΙΩΝ or ΓΕΘΧΙΑΝ—which is just nothing.   The silver has been snapped in the
thinnest part of the circumference.

Wednesday, 29th Dec.—A party of us set
out early this morning on a shooting excursion,
being tempted by certain incorrect accounts of
abundance of game.   With me, however, this
was only a minor object ; I was sure to see the
country, and that was as much as I cared
about.

There is little variety in this part of Attica ;
mountains dotted with the cypress and myrtle
and obtruding sharp edges of rock at every
step make much walking a very painful exertion : but the scenery is of so novel a character
that it cannot avoid giving pleasure to the pe-
destrian, however inconvenienced he may be
by the numerous obstacles which impede his
way.   A short distance to the south is a small
plain upon which are some cedars, and a well
of good water which furnishes supplies for the
neighbourhood.   Here I found a considerable
herd of small cattle and ponies, watched by
several Greeks armed, and attended by their
black wolf-dogs.   They were fine-looking ani-

mals, but savage in the extreme. A Greek
who had shot a number of small birds offered
me the produce of his bag for a little gun-
powder; but being rather apprehensive that
by complying I might arm him against myself,
should he take a fancy to any thing I carried,
I declined his request, and he seemed a good
deal disappointed. Perhaps I did him an in-
justice, and especially as he knew that the
Cambrian lay close by, and would therefore
hardly have made any hostile attempt. In
another part of this plain they were ploughing
with oxen, presenting the only signs of cultivation that I discovered. The wood in many
parts has been subjected to fire, but for what
purpose is not very apparent; probably to
cook the food of the cow-herds as they attend
upon their charge. To the north of the plain
rises the highest point in the country, affording
a very beautiful and extended prospect. I
traversed several deep ravines before I reached
it, and ascended with considerable difficulty:
before reaching the main summit I found a
level ground abounding in long-forsaken mine-
shafts, and great quantities of scoriæ—here
were the silver mines of Ancient Attica:—the

Negropont—Scio—Massacre of the Greeks.

whole of the upper strata appeared of white marble; I distinguished also a few pine-trees among the heights, but they were more abundant below.

Thursday, 30th Dec.—At one o'clock this morning we made sail, leaving Negropont, the ancient Eubœa, on the left.

> " Eubœa next her martial sons prepares,
> And sends the brave Abantes to the wars:
> Breathing revenge, in arms they take their way
> From Chalcis' walls and strong Eretria *."

Such were they in the Homeric age. Chalcis, now Negropont, is still the capital of the island, but the " Strong Eretria," I believe, exists only in its name. We had much wind throughout the day.

Friday, 31st Dec.—About noon we left Scio, (anciently Chios) on our right; it is called by the Turks " the Mastic Island" from the abundance of that tree, which it produces; but it is better known of late by the infamous butchery of the Greeks about five years since. Amongst the multitude of sufferers was my

* Pope's Homer, B. II.

present servant, a lad of about fourteen years
of age; his father was murdered, himself and
three younger brothers were taken prisoners
and confined in separate ships, where the Turks
busied themselves in attempting their conversion. How they succeeded with the other
lads does not appear; but Nicholai, (the boy in
my service) was soon after transferred to the
English corvette, Martin, Captain Eden, from
whence he came last voyage to the Cambrian.
He has forgotten nothing of his native language, and speaks tolerable English. The
poor fellow's mother, the only being connected
with him, of whose existence he has heard, resides at Smyrna, where he will probably see
her for the first time since the slaughter of
their countrymen. He has been long enough
in England to become attached to it, and very
naturally prefers security and enjoyment there
to the perils and barbarities of which Greece
has been the seat. On our left appeared the
island of Ipsara, not less remarkable than Scio
for having been the scene of the Greek revolution.

Saturday, January 1st, 1825, NEW-YEAR'S-
DAY.—I was awakened soon after midnight by

the sound of music, and presently I heard a loud knock at my cabin-door: not anticipating any such salutation in a man of war, I could not collect myself soon enough to return the " happy new year," which a voice from without bestowed on me. But it broke my sleep, and brought on a train of those reflections, which it is perhaps the wisdom of every man to welcome on the opening of a new year.

As I retraced the events of the last twelve-month I saw much occasion for regret : I found that I had " followed too much the devices and desires of my own heart ;" and that many things had been left undone which it was my duty to do. Alas ! how often in the course of a man's life will such reflections arise, and how often will they be turned aside and blunted by worldly pleasure and ambition ! The current of time is frequently checked by the impediments and restraints of conscience, but it rushes on, rising higher and higher, till the opposing mound is swept away and hurried into the common vortex of oblivion. As pebbles in the stream are the penitentiary regrets of human life—there is a little additional bubble—a momentary tarriance of the waters of

11

error, and then all flows on smooth and untroubled as before! My mind recurred to the land of my nativity, with

" Thoughts of many, and with fears for some."

Surrounded by the ocean, which dashed against the sides of my cabin, and separated by thousands of miles from that community to which I had been so long accustomed and attached, I felt all the uncertainty natural to the situation in which I was placed.

" My friends!—do they now and then send
    A wish or a thought after me,
To tell me, I yet have a friend,—
    Tho' a friend whom I never may see ?"

There is nothing which so much soothes and quiets the heart as the belief that some one is interested in its welfare. But then, when I recollect how many, who called themselves my friends in the early spring of youthful affection, have become estranged, and, to all moral purposes, dead to me; when I recal the various chances which may be busy in estranging others,—the retrospect almost paralyzes hope, and deadens the activity of every kindly feeling.. The friends of my childhood are scattered over the world; some of them perhaps deceased :——I know nothing of their fate. The friends of a more advanced age appear but as those who linger on the confines of eternity, as if about to bid a last adieu to the reciprocity of early attachment. Those of the other sex with whom I have had intimacy and correspondence—for youth is indiscriminate in its friendships, and feels not the danger that it does not see,—have, one by one, fallen from the list : " star after star decays," and the remembrance of the mild and beautiful light which they afforded, is a source of just regret, while it argues not much for the permanency of those to come. There was change of situation and of pursuits, and of ideas arising from both. Well, at least, I have made other friends ; they have been tried, and have not been found wanting,—at least, I believe so. The mind is a plastic thing, and soon associates itself with new forms, and receives new impressions. If they be not so strong, perhaps they are as durable. We grow more careful as we grow older ; and observing the fragility of these fine porcelain vases of humanity, we touch them with a lighter hand, and use them but on rare occasions.

For the future,—for the "*new year,*" will it be "*happy?*" Yes, if it be virtuous. We are less dependent creatures than we believe—less the children of circumstance than we wish to suppose ourselves. An undeviating rectitude of character, a strong and rooted principle of religion, will create and then multiply felicity in every varied stage of existence. Like the diamond, religion carries light along with it. It is bright even in " utter darkness," yet let but a beam of temporal prosperity shine there, and mark how gloriously it will sparkle! Without it, the treasure is to the full as valuable; the diamond is equally costly; but then the world's eye overpasses it, and, overpassing it, men fancy that the thing does not really exist! How false and how foolish a mode of estimating worth! The fable of the cock and the jewel, in Æsop, can only be its parallel.

The sun rose magnificently this morning, as if celebrating the birth-day of a new year. It gilded the mountains at the entrance of the Gulf of Smyrna, and it irradiated the sea in one long glowing volume. So shines the " Sun of Righteousness" upon those who follow his course.

As we passed up the gulf, a vast number of sea-birds were seen disporting themselves; amongst which were pelicans and swans. The latter are rare at this period of the year; but in summer they are numerous. A string of camels were reposing upon the shore; and, as the first indication of another continent, even at this distance, gave considerable life to the prospect. We passed a Turkish fort, of singular construction, which commands the bay; and observed huge granite balls lying upon the beach *in terrorem*, I suppose. A fair wind brought us presently to Smyrna, where we found the Seringapatam, and, before long, the dragoman, an Armenian interpreter, (of which nation the interpreters generally are,) came on board. The dress of the Armenians is peculiar. They wear a sort of high cap, somewhat resembling a double pair of boxing gloves, meeting one another in friendly embrace. A silk or cotton vest, covered by a cloak of ample sleeves, forms also part of their array. With the first opportunity I went on shore, and wandered at random among the narrow and dirty streets of

Smyrna. When the Cambrian was last here, it might not have been so safe. An officer of the ship, who was in her at the time, having occasion to go on shore, observed a Turk assault a Greek, and, at a single blow, strike off his head, which he seized, and bore away with him : the carcase was left in the street. The Levite and Mahommedan saw and " passed by," with indifference, " on the other side." For this act of barbarity, there was no investigation, and no punishment. The unruly passions of a Turkish mob were aroused; and no sense, either of duty or of decency, could suspend the malevolent and wanton expression.

We had, this morning, an alarm respecting the plague. Three or four infected persons, it was said, had arrived at Smyrna a short time previously; and our captain was justly apprehensive of the consequences. Happily, however, the report, so far as it regarded the period of their being brought here, was false. It occurred several months before, and every customary precaution had been taken with effect. The disorder never spread further.

The streets of Smyrna are scarcely three yards in breadth; and of this the greater part is taken up by a puddle, which finds a channel through the whole. Strings of camels take their way through them, splashing and crushing the passenger to his heart's content. And should it be his fortune, as it is more than probable, to meet a Turk mounted upon the sprightly little coursers of the country, he may esteem himself marvellously happy, should he escape without being blinded by the mud that he fails not to splash about him. But these are little Asiatic luxuries, for which an inquisitive traveller cannot be too thankful! In my first wanderings, the most marked circumstance was the corpse-like appearance of the Turkish women, muffled up in white cotton shawls, from top to toe, with a piece of thin black crape, like the aventagle of a helmet, enveloping the face; they seem to have just started from the sepulchre, and to wander, like Goules, in search of prey. Some of these masks have holes cut for the eyes in the crape, which, in that part, is covered with gauze, so as to permit their seeing with more distinctness, but yet entirely to exclude all prospect from without. In this manner they go, three or four in company, to the bazars.

Above the city, to the right, is the ancient Mount Pagus, crowned by a castle once of immense extent, but now completely buried in ruins. The colossal head of the Amazon Smyrna is fixed in the wall at the North gate, divested both of nose and lips. Chandler, Tournefort, and other writers, have given long and accurate accounts of the antiquities of this place and neighbourhood. To them, therefore, I refer my readers, contenting myself with remarking only whatever is novel, or more than commonly striking. Difference of situation or circumstance may, perhaps, put some things in another and happier light; but to transcribe long and dry details of antiquity from one or all the writers who have indulged in them, would, indeed, augment the body of matter, but be, I apprehend, neither amusing nor instructive. From the walls of the castle we have a splendid panoramic view of the country around Smyrna, ornamented with olive-trees and orange groves. To the left, is the gulf, with English, French, Austrian, and Dutch ships of war, riding at anchor. In front, the town with its Moschs and Minarets, its " cities of the dead," indicated by stately groves of cypress-trees, lifting themselves aloft in gloomy majesty : the river Meles winding gracefully past various picturesque Turkish residences ; and higher up, the rough stony road to Bour-navat and Boujah, over which a long string of camels, with bells round their necks that chime harmoniously in the distance, preserve their slow uniform pace. Mountains, slightly covered with verdure, surround and terminate the scene.

The burial-places are numerous and re-markable. Wherever a dead body is found, there it is interred ; and as Turkish superstition will not permit a second burial to take place where there has been one before, the country is covered with these tokens of mortality. Cypresses are invariably planted near them ; and the passenger may distinguish the rank of the deceased by the stone turban which is placed on the head of the monument. These are frequently painted and gilded ; and but for the solemn gloom of the tree which shadows them, would have an unseemly and garish ap-pearance. Texts of the Koran are inscribed upon each. In their turbans, the Turks, as well as the Greek inhabitants of Smyrna, especially the women, frequently place anemones and other gay flowers. The effect is very pleasing; and might seem to point out a taste more refined, and a feeling more delicate, than usually accompanies either one or the other. There is a cotton print manufacture at Smyrna of great extent. The cottons come from England, and when printed, are exported to Russia, France, and other countries. The process is probably similar to our own.

I had an adventure to-day which might have terminated unhappily. Walking leisurely along one of the streets appropriated to the Frank residents, and hence called *Frank-street,* I passed two Turks, armed as they all are with pistols and ataghan. I observed that one if not both of them was drunk; but I paid little further attention to them. However, I had not proceeded far, before I saw half a dozen Greek boys running rapidly before me, turning their heads back with every mark of consternation. This action naturally induced me to turn mine, when, to my great annoyance, I perceived one of the drunken Turks aforesaid, with his cocked pistol presented at my back. I had scarcely determined what to do, when his companion interfered; and placing himself before him, pushed him gently round the corner of the street near which they stood. They disappeared not faster than I did : I felt not the least *penchant* for that sort of villainous entertainment.

Tuesday, 4th Jan.—I entered a Mosch, which I shall describe.—The entrance of each of these buildings is furnished with a fountain, and a number of cocks. The worshipper here makes his ablutions; he washes his feet, hands, breast, and face; then rinses his mouth, and wipes all upon a handkerchief or shawl which he carries in his bosom. Ascending a few steps, a stone pavement, which is covered with mats, leads into the Mosch. On this matted ground, the slippers of the Moslem are deposited as he proceeds into the building. Some of them, however, first worship without before they enter; and others, but fewer, go no further at the time. The Mosch is covered with carpeting laid upon mats to preserve it from the friction of the stone beneath. The East side facing the entrance has a profusion of gilding, with verses from the Koran inscribed in the centre. Save that there is no com-

munion-table, the resemblance of the gingerbread work of a Roman Catholic church is not
inconsiderable.   On each side of this showy
part, a pulpit is erected; one of which the
iman ascends by a staircase of white marble;
all beside is painted in imitation of it.   Fronting
the pulpits is a wooden gallery; and in the
centre circular rows of lamps are suspended.
When the worshipper enters, he stands erect,
looking towards the shrine, if it may be so
called.   By and by he bows his body horizon-
tally; then his knees bend until they gradually
touch the ground, by which movement his
head (or rather nose) pretty much at the same
time is also brought in contact with it.   He
again stands erect, and is continually repeating
the same process, till he finishes his devotional
exercise.   There is generally some one or other
engaged in these ridiculous rites; and whatever dissimilarity there may be between their
professions and actions, they certainly appear
in earnest when they enter the Mosch.

A singular instance of a Turk's confidence
in an Englishman occurred to-day.   The chaplain of the Seringapatam passing through the
bazar, was attracted to a Turkish shop, and

shewn a fine rose diamond which had been part of the plunder of the unfortunate island of Scio. The Turk asked a considerable sum, but stated himself no judge of the value. "Are you," said he, "an Englishman?" He replied, through his interpreter, in the affirmative, and added, that he was an officer of an English frigate. "Then take the ring," said the Turk, "and keep it a day or two; get some one to examine it, and judge by that means of its value—I have no apprehension that an Englishman will deceive me." The ring was taken, and afterwards bought for 20l. but the gentleman who was thus trusted had never (that he knew of) been seen by the seller, nor could the latter have any knowledge of him, except, perhaps, that he really was an Englishman. The fact deserves record, even though another inference should be drawn from it.

On returning to the ship, I enquired of the Greek whose boat I employed, why he did not join his countrymen in their struggle for freedom? The man appeared to feel the question with considerable liveliness, and replied " that he knew it was his duty, but that he had a family of small children who must perish if he

13

left them, for that they would be at once exposed to Turkish cruelty and to extreme want *." The Greek government would doubtless do well could they provide, in some way, for the families of those who enter their service, and assure them of their utmost protection. They cannot otherwise expect, under present circumstances, that their countrymen will cooperate zealously and firmly in the cause. It is currently reported here, that the Greeks have cut out a Turkish schooner of war and three merchant vessels laden with oil from Mitylene, a few days since.

Wednesday, 5th Jan.—Though this morning was somewhat rainy I dedicated it to the inspection of two aqueducts thrown over the river Meles, one at the foot of Mount Pagus, and the other at the distance of two miles. The edges of the river are beautifully fringed with the Laurea Rosa, which marks the course of the stream for a considerable distance :

---

* My Greek master a few days after this alleged as a reason for his not joining the league, that they were so divided amongst themselves as to render it unwise and useless to serve them. No man wants reasons for what he dislikes ; but I fear that there is too much truth in his allegation.

mountains rise on each side of it.   The further
aqueduct is composed of two structures united,
and is of much greater antiquity than the
other; its situation is finely romantic.   The
river Meles supplies water to a variety of mills
which are built upon its banks.   Drummond,
in his volume of Travels, has given drawings of
both these aqueducts, but they are as unlike as
they can possibly be; although he has, as he
says, " *what they call a tradesman's eye* *,"
mean what it may, it certainly deceived him :
the representations which he has given have a
greater resemblance to spouts than to the aqueducts of Smyrna.   It rained heavily whilst I
remained here.   Returning by the castle, I observed the last perishing ruins of the ancient
amphitheatre, buried as nearly as may be in
the soil.   The barbarians have carried off whatever they could lay hands on for domestic
uses; and the rest will be soon overwhelmed
by the rapidly accumulating dust.   Other
ruins, by some called the Church of St. Poly-
carp, by others the Temple of Janus—(" they
smell as sweet" by one name as by the other,

* Drummond's Travels, fol. p. 115. 1754.

and perhaps are equally appropriate)——are also hastening to total annihilation; and it will soon be said of them, "*etiam periere ruinæ.*"

Thursday, 6th Jan.——This being Christmas-day with the Greek Catholics, their churches are adorned in the gayest manner. I entered one, in which a sort of raree-show had been set up, illumed with a multitude of candles: the subject of it was the birth of Christ, who was represented in the back ground, by a little waxen figure wrapped up in embroidery, and reclining upon an embroidered cushion, which rested upon another of pink satin: this was *supposed* to be the manger where he was born. Behind the image two paper bulls' heads looked unutterable things. On the right was the Virgin Mary, and on the left one of the Eastern Magi. Paper clouds, in which the paper heads of numberless cherubs appeared, enveloped the whole; while from a paste-board cottage stalked a wooden monk, with dogs, and sheep, and camels, goats, lions, and lambs; here walked a maiden upon a stratum of sods and dried earth, and there a shepherd, flourishing aloft his pastoral staff. The construction of these august figures was [chiefly Dutch: they were

intermixed with china images and miserable
daubs on paper.   In the centre, a real fountain
in miniature squirted forth water to the in-
effable delight of crowds of " prostrate worshippers."

Friday, 7th Jan.——Wandering through one
part of the bazar, I was struck with the cries
of the venders of merchandize.   Amongst other
things a fine diamond ring and a Turkey carpet
were exposed for sale.   These, and especially
the latter, reminded me of the magical carpet
of Hossein, in the Arabian Tales, where the
mode of sale is exactly similar.

Monday, 10th Jan.——Introduced this morning to the Rev. Fr. V. Arundell, chaplain to
the factory here.   A Greek lady, whom I met
at his house, pronounced the ring which I formerly mentioned to have been found at Athens
an antique ; how far she was a judge is not
clear—is *rather* doubtful ! Mr. Arundell shewed
me a number of queries sent by the Bible Society to their agent here, and purporting to
relate to an object which the Society are said
to have in view——the conversion of the Jews in
Smyrna :——amongst other pertinent questions,
are,

" The nature of the water, and how to be corrected?

" The unhealthy winds, and how to be avoided?

" What are the usual *condiments* used in diet?

" Is it best to take out *bills* or *cash* from Malta?

" The best hours for sleep, food, exercise and study?

" What is the best season for a stranger to arrive in the country?"

With others of a similar character, which have just as much to do with the " conversion of the Jews" as with the man in the moon. It strikes me very forcibly that some " ready writer," intending to get up a volume of travels, or peradventure, twain, has adopted this mode of acquiring information. It would cost the agent of the Society months of hard labour and minute investigation to reply accurately to many of the questions.

As soon as we arrived we received invitations to the balls of the Casino, which take place once a week, and continue to the end of the Carnival, and " to which," (Mr. Hobhouse observes) " all the respectable Greeks and ladies of their families are invited." But I am informed that the ladies are rather Smyrniotes than Greeks; that is, born in Smyrna, but of Frank extraction. They adopt indeed the Greek dress, and unbecoming enough it is, except the small *turban*, which is worn sideways upon the head, and has a tasteful air; but the little jackets, *Grecian bend*, and STAYS-LESS form can never be tolerated by Europeans, properly so called; and the postures into which they throw themselves, especially after being heated with dancing, in any but a native must be pronounced positively indecent and disgusting. In corpulent matrons this feeling is, of course, still stronger; and it is surprizing, if they are not altogether or in part of Greek origin, how this dress could ever have been adopted.

Several of the officers dined to-day with the English consul—here was the first *tendour* that I had seen. This is a square table covered with thick carpet; beneath, on a sort of shelf lined with tin, is a chafing-dish containing hot charcoal, and on this shelf people put their feet during cold weather, enveloping their knees in the carpet.

CHAPTER V.

====

TUESDAY, 11*th Jan.*——Captain Hamilton presented his officers to Hassan Capitan Pacha of Smyrna. These sort of interviews have not been so often, or so accurately described as to render recapitulation tedious; I shall therefore detail, with some degree of minuteness, what has just taken place. We left the ship in five boats, the captain in the first yawl, with the union jack flying at her head, the rest of the boats following with pendants; the Dragoman and the English consul, with his janizaries were in a sixth.

We entered a dark and dirty court-yard, up an ascent equally villainous. Musquets and carbines were reclining against a wall, and a number of uncouth retainers were smoaking near them. Crossing a sort of hall, at the top of the stair-case, where lay a multitude of slippers, and where certain fierce-looking mussulmans were pacing to and fro, we were ushered into a square matted chamber, of no very considerable extent. The ceiling and half the wainscot were plainly painted : the Eastern end being daubed in sorrowful imitation of marble, and inscribed in the upper part with a sentence from the Koran. To the right of the door, which occupied a corner of the room, were other texts, with a banner, on the top of which the crescent was depicted. In a corner of the left-hand wall, carbines and huge powder-flasks were suspended. A low couch, called a *divan*, covered with silk, surrounded the apartment in the usual manner. Dirty cotton sun-blinds excluded the light on one side, and a sort of Venetian shutter, partly elevated and partly closed, rose from without, on the other. In the most distant corner of the chamber, and exactly opposite to the entrance, sat the Capitan Pacha, wrapped in a furred cloak. A sabre and belt hung on his right hand, and a telescope lay on a ledge of the window upon his left. Such was the arrangement of the audience chamber !

The Pacha himself was a fine-looking man, apparently middle aged, with a keen expres-

sion of countenance.   His brow was high and
falling, with large bushy eye-brows, remarkably
arched, and approximating so nearly as almost
to meet : when he frowned, this must have
taken place.   His eyes were small and pro-
jecting, but quick; and indicating a man of
much natural observation and intellect. An ac-
quiline nose, long mustachios, and a dark
curling beard, gave considerable character to
the expression of his thin and embrowned
features.

When we were seated, the dragoman opened
the conference; in the course of which, we
heard several unoriental bursts of merriment.
He appeared, indeed, in the very best mood.
Soon after our arrival, began the clatter of
coffee-cups ; and this favourite beverage, both
of Turk and Frank, was then presented to
each individual in a silver or brass case, of the
same form as the cup denominated *zarff :* it
is intended to serve the purpose of our saucers.
By and by came immense long pipes, made
of the cherry-stick, with amber and enameled
mouth-pieces.   The pipe-head is made either
of plain or gilded clay, and rests, when smoked,
upon a brazen dish, placed at the distance of

several yards on the floor. Then came the tug
of war. As Campbell saith, not indeed on an
occasion *quite* similar,

> " 'Tis morn;—but scarce yon level sun
> Can pierce the smoke-clouds rolling dun,
> Where fiery Frank, and furious Hun,
> Prate in their sulphury canopy."

From the mouth of the Pacha, " bearded
like a Pard," the smoke issued, as I have seen
it from a cottage chimney in a wood, gradually
making its way above the tops of the tallest
trees, and winding in many an airy volume
through the intersecting branches. But it was
yet a more whimsical sight to observe the
younger of the midshipmen strenuously endeavouring to do justice to the Pacha's entertainment. Imagine a chamber of twenty to
thirty feet square, with low couches on three
of the sides, where sat a host of lads in cocked
hats, swords by their sides, and pipes at least
six feet long in their mouths : conceive their
grimaces, their ill-concealed smiles, breaking
from beneath the flimsy texture of gravity
with which they struggled to veil their mirth ;
and, at intervals, breathing forth clouds of

smoke! Conceive this, and behold the levee of the Pacha!

When the first pipe was concluded, a second was brought, with an additional cup of coffee, and a glass of sherbet, which is nothing more than lemonade. While we were smoking, the Pacha's band played without; and if the reader ever heard a troop of children in the hilarity of their hearts squeaking lustily forth from penny trumpets, and beating sixpenny drums, they will have the exactest possible idea of the music with which we were regaled. We sat rather more than an hour, and then retired to pay a visit to Suleiman Aga, collector of the customs. Here, though there was less state, there was more comfort. The arrangement of our reception and entertainment, was pretty much the same. The Aga was in the midst of papers, and two or three secretaries sat on the divan beside him. He lamented that he could shew us no other mark of civility than that of " offering a bitter pipe and a cup of coffee." But he hoped we would visit him at his country house, and the following Sunday was accordingly fixed upon for that purpose. Whilst we remained, he signed and sealed a packet, which

13

the dragoman had requested him to forward
to Constantinople, on mercantile affairs. The
signature was effected by passing a small
camel-hair brush, moistened with ink, over a
signet : it was then stamped upon the paper,
and restored to the gold thread purse from
whence it was taken. It was scarcely done,
when a Turk entered, arrayed in the sacred
green, which marks the descent from Moham-
med. This was no other than Hassan, the
ci-devant Pacha and compassionate Governor
of Scio, when the ever memorable massacre
of the islanders took place!

   We were, this evening, at a crowded ball at
Mr. Whittle's, (what odious names these people
have,) a Smyrna merchant. Mr. Strangways
informed me, that he had here discovered the
pepper-custard of the Arabian Tales. I was
not so fortunate as to detect him ; so I resign
all the honour to the Honourable.

   Wednesday, 12th Jan.—By the great kindness of the Rev. Mr. Arundell, I had an opportunity of seeing a good deal of the neighbourhood of Smyrna: having been invited on
a shooting excursion to that gentleman's house
at Sedecui. Asses were ordered, but the day

first selected not agreeing with our convenience, we fixed on the day after.   The consequence of which was, that the owner of our
donkies refused to permit us to employ them,
or rather promised in order to deceive us. The
man was a Greek, and our worthy host would
fain have had me believe, that it was a specimen of that obstinacy and pride which he said
was characteristic of the nation.   The worst of
it was, that the fellows who let asses out to
hire are so leagued together, that by offending
one, you offend the whole ; at least our efforts
to obtain more than two beasts for our lug-
gage, were quite ineffectual. Notwithstanding,
I am resolved to suffer nothing but a series of
irresistible facts, of facts fairly and impartially
chosen, to induce me to form an unfavourable
opinion of those who have so much to contend
with.   They fight for freedom ; they fight with
years of slavery upon their backs, with all the
necessary vices of slavery, and with some
arising immediately from intercourse with
their enslavers ;—let them have fair play !

    The country around Sedecui is diversified
with hill and dale, abounding in underwood,
but with few trees of any growth. The Velania

oak, the myrtle, &c. &c. are common to all
these parts. The olive seems to flourish most;
—the pine less. Game is not very plentiful at
present. The cold weather having prevailed
for several days, it was expected that wood-
cocks would have been numerous. This was
not the case; and hares and partridges were
very scarce. A large hyæna was killed a short
time since, near Sedecui; but such an event is
of extraordinary occurrence. A report goes
abroad, that tigers, and even *bears*, have been
seen here: I am a little incredulous.

At the breaking out of the Greek Revolution,
Sedecui suffered severely by the march of the
Turkish troops to Scala Nova, for the purpose
of attacking Samos. A Turkish officer and
his follower, during the night that a detach-
ment was quartered here, pursued a young
Greek girl along the streets. She took refuge
in the house of a countrywoman, and closed
the door in sufficient time to escape by another
entrance. The Turk at last got admission;
and finding that the victim had eluded his
brutal grasp, prepared to wreak his vengeance
upon her helpless protector. He raised his
arm to strike her to the heart; but, strange to

say, the sabre snapt asunder at the hilt, while it was lifted in the air. He then directed a pistol at her, but here again he was foiled—it missed fire! This being observed by his comrade, he forced him away, remarking, happily for the woman, "*that her hour was not yet come.*" Resolved, however, not to be wholly defeated, he seized upon a fine infant, which then lay sleeping in its cradle beside her, and rushed out of the house. In vain the half-frantic mother called upon the ruffian to restore her offspring; in vain she supplicated him to have compassion upon her agony: she obtained nothing but savage imprecations and menaces, and such was the disorderly state of the Turkish army, that the Capitan Pacha himself had no power to compel a surrender. In fact, the man had taken a liking to the child, and persisted in retaining him. This, however, was ultimately prevented by direction of the commander. They removed the boy while the ravisher slept; and the effects of his resentment were provided against, by marching immediately to their next destination, where the Greeks were beyond his reach. The singularly providential escape of the woman is attested by the most respectable authorities, and is universally credited.

I was particularly struck at Sedecui with the classical contour of a Greek servant of our host. A white shawl was bound across her head, and fastened under the chin. The effect of this costume, though not common with her countrywomen, was augmented by a long antique lamp, which she carried on the occasion I speak of, made at Venice, but admirably adapted to carry back the imagination to remoter periods, and more heroic times.

Near Sedecui is a tumulus, which has not yet been explored; the French call it the tomb of Andræmon; and they might as well call it the tomb of Jack the Giant Queller! Mr. Arundell, whose antiquarian research equals the friendliness of his manners, proposes, in quieter times, to investigate the tumulus in question, as well as an opposite mound about a mile distant. It gives me pleasure also to mention, that he has it in contemplation to communicate to the public the result of certain well-conducted enquiries relative to the ancient Christian churches of Asia. He has recovered several curious and valuable monuments, and from the ardour of his pursuit, united as it is with great discretion and judgment, I have no doubt but his object will be fully attained.

We returned to Smyrna by Bougiah, otherwise called "the English village," from the number of its English inhabitants: it is about three miles from the city. A curious circumstance happened here a short time since; the lower floor of a large house has been converted into a chapel—a man, carrying a bowl of milk, stood accidentally beneath the door-way of the building, and a serpent, four or five feet long, allured by the smell of the milk, of which they are extremely fond, darted from the upper part of the door, and flung himself, like a necklace, around the throat of the poor fellow. The creature's head was dipped into the bowl; and one may well imagine the terror of his entertainer, and the little satisfaction which he would receive from the " orient carcanet" with which he was decorated. Whether the serpent was of a harmless description, which is most probable, or whether the man contrived, by a vigorous effort, to free himself from the uncourteous intruder, I did not hear—certain it is that he escaped without injury. I would add

to this account that many of the tales of the
" GESTA ROMANORUM *" and of other books
of that class, are founded upon the propensity
of serpents for milk; and this very circumstance, perhaps, is no small proof of their
Eastern origin.

Friday, 14th Jan.—We returned to-day,
and found that Suleiman Aga and his suite had
been paying a visit to the Cambrian. Amongst
the rest, the late Pacha of Scio, who to his
other admirable qualities adds that of a confirmed drunkard, was present. He honoured
Captain Hamilton with a——kiss on each cheek.
Such a mark of civility was a thing " devoutly
to be wished," and, I doubt not, duly appre-
ciated by our excellent captain! Indeed I cannot help shrewdly suspecting that the second
salute was effected by stratagem ; and that
when he had been smacked upon one side " he
turned to him the other also !"

Sunday, 16th Jan.—After morning service,
Captain Hamilton, Mr. Tennant, the Hon. Mr.
Strangways, &c. fifteen of the officers of the

* See Tale LXI. Vol. II. of the Translated *Gesta* amongst
others.

Cambrian, and nine or ten from the Seringa-patam, with their commander, went, according to appointment, to dine with Suleiman Aga, at his country-house. This was considered so rare an instance of attention as to cause a good deal of commotion in Smyrna, a like circum-stance never having been heard of even by the oldest Frank inhabitants. But Captain Ha-milton is so much and so justly esteemed; he has adopted, since his first arrival in the Medi-terranean, a policy so well conceived and judi-ciously supported, that there is little to surprize if we find the Turks themselves discarding their prejudices, and admitting even " Christian dogs" to the familiarity of their houses—and a most singular gratification we received. On landing at the consul's we found horses await-ing our arrival; many of them were superbly caparisoned, and their high-peaked saddles and gorgeous trappings were strongly contrasted with the costume of the English riders. They were fine little animals, and their spirit was kept in continual heat by the awkward use of the *shovel-stirrup*, a huge instrument sharpened at each end, and employed as a spur. With this some of our cavalcade unwittingly gored the poor animals till the blood ran profusely down its elevated edges.

When the bustle of mounting was over we set forward to the Aga's residence, in as much order as the restlessness of the animals we bestrode would admit. It was diverting to observe the efforts made by some of the officers to quiet their steeds, in order to keep their persons in equilibrio as we proceeded up the narrow and dirty streets of Smyrna. The puddle flew about us most mischievously, and not the less that we were regarded by hundreds of faces " from doors and windows, yea, from chimney tops." The Greek ladies have not more curiosity, perhaps, than the rest of their sex, but their turbaned heads, enwreathing dark hair adorned with natural flowers of the brightest colours, and eyes and cheeks smiling like the sun of their own glorious land, looked out with all the inquisitiveness of excited wonder. By the side of each horse a Turk ran as a guard, and an armed janizary on horseback, with about a dozen on foot, preceded the cavalcade.

The Aga's dwelling being but a short distance from the town we were soon there, pass-

ing in the way the river Meles, over which a
bridge, called the *Caravan Bridge*, has been
thrown, adjacent to a fine grove of cypress.   A
magnificent band welcomed our arrival! It
was composed of three fiddles, a dulcimer, a
triangle, and an oaten pipe ;—I need not say
what the music was *like!* Dismounting in the
area of the building we ascended by a flight of
steps, and were ushered into a long hall, of
which a square basin of water formed the
centre ; along its sides, pillars, imitative of
marble, supported a gilded roof.   To the left,
where the Aga and his retinue waited to receive
us, the floor was raised and boarded, and was
partly inclosed by a marble balustrade : a low
sofa (or divan,) covered with printed cotton,
ran on each side, that is to say, at the end and
on two adjoining sides ; the fourth was open,
looking toward the basin, and a similar place
in the opposite portion of the building.   A
large glass chandelier was suspended at each
end ; and the ceiling, as well as the wainscot,
was painted in tolerably good style.   On each
side of the first-mentioned part was a little
chamber, secured by a door, and in one of
these, to the right of the entrance, the Aga was

fitting up an English fire-place of well-executed marble. All the rooms were painted.

The further end of the building (which, as I have already hinted, was open, affording an uninterrupted prospect of its whole length, with the basin in the midst) was raised and boarded, like the other; but before reaching it, a marble fountain, with a number of jets d'eau, were to be observed. To the left of this a door opened upon a small terrace or balcony, which presented a beautiful view of the adjoining country, its olive-groves and mountains swelling magnificently beyond.

After being presented and seated we were supplied with pipes and cold punch, and having inhaled a few whiffs, the Aga proposed that we should walk through his house and gardens. This, of course, was gladly acquiesced in, and we accordingly set forth. The house I have already described. We were presently conducted through a green trelliced walk covered with branches of the vine, at the termination of which were vapour-baths and the harem. In the former we saw little remarkable; they were small but conveniently enough contrived; a flat stone was inserted in the boarded floor,

on which the body reclines while the vapour is
in circulation.   From hence—which I take to
be of itself an instance of special favour—we
were brought to the HAREM.   The women, it
is scarcely necessary to remark, had been removed, but I apprehend that few Turks are
tempted, under any circumstance, to make exhibition even of their empty cages.   However
this may be, we were gratified by an inspection
of places guarded with the most scrupulous
vigilance, and made the vehicle of the most
monstrous system that ever disgraced civilized
humanity !   The ground part of the building
was at this time unappropriated, indeed was
unfinished, but ascending a flight of steps,
screened by a narrow lattice, we came into the
women's apartments.   In this quarter they remain during the heats of the morning, but as
the evening advances they retire to the upper
chambers, where they also sleep.   Each story
consists of three rooms, or rather two rooms and
a little square place partitioned from the corridor,
but open to it.   The partition itself is not more
than three feet high.   The sleeping apartments
are boarded, leaving a lower space at the entrance for the purpose of discarding dirty slippers

before the carpet is approached. The same quarter of the room is also allotted to a variety of wardrobes, and little closets for depositing trinkets and other articles of female attire. They occupy the whole breadth of the chamber. Opposite, and along the adjacent sides are the beds, above which numerous glass windows, with moveable lattices fitted to them, admit the air while they prevent the exposure of their persons. The prospect from hence is beautiful; and provided that they who are thus immured can survey the wide and magnificent expanse of heaven above, can see the flowers freely blooming beneath them, and the feathered creation fluttering in liberty and joy around them, without a sigh, they may perhaps taste enjoyment even here!

From the harem we proceeded to the garden adjoining. This, (as well as the buildings,) has not been long constructed; it was therefore, in its present state, no very attractive object, consisting entirely of young trees and vegetables in abundance. We passed a well of curious though simple form; a large wheel (to which a multitude of small leather buckets were attached) was fixed in it; as the wheel revolved part of the buckets arose filled with water whilst the remainder were filling below. Each, as it arrived at the summit of the well, emptied its contents into a reservoir which was connected with small aqueducts built on either side of the beds in the garden. A short distance from hence the Aga's house and harem formed very picturesque objects. The dresses of the British navy intermingling with the shewy costume of Turks, Greeks and Armenians, all illumined too by the splendour of an Eastern sun, made a novel and interesting appearance.

The stables of the Aga were next inspected ; they contained probably upwards of an hundred horses of burden, besides numbers destined only for the saddle. This building forms one wall of the area before his house, to which we now returned. Immediately small round tables were brought, upon which the attendants placed salvers of fruits, anchovies, and other *piquant* dishes, which were but the prelude to the coming entertainment. I observed the Aga, as the utmost mark of civility that he could shew, strike his tooth-pick into part of a pear already separated from the rind, and pre-

sent it with much politesse to his nearest guests.
What was the *flavour* of this pear I never asked,
nor do I pretend to guess, but " by the foot
of Pharaoh !" as Captain Bobadil says, (peradventure Pharaoh's *tooth* here were the more
appropriate attestation !) I felt not, nor feel
the least envy at their happiness ! A worthy
personage who partook of it solemnly assured
me that the Aga used this aforesaid tooth-pick
in the common way, not only afterward, but
before the presentation. Far be it from me
to impugn the veracity of this worthy personage, but as no one beside witnessed the exhibition *, (and I took considerable pains to
ascertain so important a fact) it rests entirely
with my readers to credit it or not. The tables,
four in number, were placed near the divan;
but as a few only could with convenience sit
at them from thence, awkwardly constructed
chairs were added. A hundred attendants at
least bustled about, bringing cold punch in

---

* This appears to have been a mistake, for Mr. Tennant
has since assured me that he particularly noticed it ; *I*
have not, therefore, the smallest doubt upon the subject ;
nor by those who have the happiness of knowing Mr. T.
will it be questioned for a moment.

VOL. I.   M

small china cups and glasses with reasonable
celerity.   A quarter of an hour afterwards the
tables were removed, and others brought.   In
this instance their disposition varied : one was
fixed up at the end where the Aga sat, and two
other in the opposite and more remote compartment ; at each of these a " familiar friend"
of our host did the honours of the table.   At
the table where I happened to be was the
aforesaid Hassan or Vehib, (for it seems he
has two appellations) *ci-devant Pacha of Scio !*
whose fawning sycophantish look corresponded
well with the unfavourable impressions which
we had long ago received. Red flabby cheeks
surmounted by small eyes that twinkled most
Bacchanalianly, and garnished with a nose as
crooked as his own soul *, is the impartial, al-

* The following anecdote is from Pouqueville's " His-
toire de la Régénération de la Grèce," a work which,
inflated and grossly incorrect as it often is, presents some
striking and veritable features of the Greek Revolution.

    " Cependant rien ne bougeait encore ; et tandis que les
Turcs préparaient leurs armes pour une expédition qui
n'était plus un mystère, un Grec, réfugié dans le consulat
de France, informé que son frère n'avait pas été compris
dans l'execution du matin, monte à la citadelle.   Il savait
qu'on devait pendre le lendemain ce qui restait encore

though not indeed an alluring description of his appearance.

We sat down: a large metal salver placed upon a small table contained a bowl of rich soup in the centre. At the edge lay a piece of bread and two spoons for the use of each individual. The bowls of the spoons were composed of tortoise-shell, the handles of ivory tipped with coral. On either side of the salver were two little dishes of custard, with two salt-cellars. VEHIB led the way by dipping his

d'otages; et il se flattait de sauver, au prix de sa tête, un père de cinq enfants qui n'avaient plus que lui pour appui et pour espérance dans cette vallée de larmes, d'où il aspirait à sortir en obtenant la couronne du martyre. Il s'etait acheminé chargé d'or et de bijoux, qu'il déposa aux pieds de Véhib Pacha, en disant: *Mon frère est ton otage, magnifique visir: daigne le rendre à sa famille. Père de cinq pauvres innocents, privés de leur mère, accorde-le à leurs larmes, en acceptant ma tête en échange de la sienne, et ces dons precieux que je te conjure d'agréer.*——*Tu seras satisfait,* repond Véhib Pacha. Il dit, et ordonnant à ses gardes d'amener le détenu: *vous allez être réunis, sortez . . . .* Puis, au mouvement d'un revers de sa main, les bourreaux, saisissant les deux victimes, font tomber leurs têtes, qu'ils rangent sur des plateaux à côté des présents que l'un d'eux venait de présenter au visir."—*Page 479, 80. Tom. III.* 1824.

spoon into the mess of soup, and inviting us by gesture to imitate him. It is not easy to express the disgust and nausea with which I prepared to follow this worthy exemplar; but at last I succeeded. An embroidered scarf of gold was suspended round each of our necks, and a napkin laid upon our knees. The soup was excellent, and so indeed it might be said of every dish that came in quick succession before us. After the soup was a roasted lamb —one of those extraordinary animals whose tail is so broad and fat and delicious, as to become an object of great importance to oriental epicures. Into this, at the invitation of our right honourable president, each man thrust his finger and tore away a piece; and thus between the spoons and the fingers alternately applied, as the nature of the dish might demand, and moistened at becoming intervals with plentiful libations of champaigne and claret, we ran through six-and-thirty dishes. To an enquiry made afterwards of the dragoman, it was said that *forty-nine* had been presented; but as I kept a careful note of what passed, I am pretty confident that I have not made a mistake. There were three tables, and the same sort of dishes exactly were brought to each, so that according to my calculation there must have been but one hundred and eight dishes; according to that of the other, one hundred and forty-seven. The curious reader may wish to know something more of this feast, which, from the rarity of the occurrence, cannot have been often mentioned; and though I am only able to afford a general idea of their component parts, yet this probably may be enough.

1. Sort of white soup, in which were a few pieces of minced liver.

2. Roasted lamb with Pistachio nuts.

3. Jelly floating on a glass bowl of water, in which gold and silver fish were swimming.

4. Roasted turkey cut in pieces, and stuffed with pine-apple seeds and peeled chesnuts.

5. Sort of white custard sprinkled with pounded cinnamon.

6. Stewed vegetables soaked in oil.

7. Custard.

8. Fried fish with an acid sauce.

9. Bread pudding sprinkled with sugar.

10. Fried fish.

11. Preserved apples with a rich syrup.

12. Grilled legs of geese.

13. Mince-meat pie with a variety of herbs, from the top of which came a living gold-finch —a common Eastern trick. It was the same at all the three tables.

14. Honied pastry.

15. Cabbage-leaves rolled up with boiled rice.

16. Almond custard.

17. Stewed chicken stuffed with pine-apple seeds.

18. Sugared cake shaped like diamonds.

19. Stewed vegetables with garlic sauce.

20. Pastry.

21. Wild boar roasted.

22. Pastry.

23. Sausages made partly with rice, herbs, &c. &c. I know not what.

24. Cakes.

25. Fried fish—mullet.

26. Cakes.

27. Wild boar or beef (I could not distinguish) done with sauce like beef-olive.

28. Melons.

29. Pastry.

30. Fried knuckles of HAM!!

31. Cakes.

32. Fritters.
33. Sort of fry with chesnuts.
34. Roasted flesh of the wild boar.
35. Large dish of boiled rice.
36. Rose-water sweetened with honey.

I should not forget to mention that VEHIB THE MERCIFUL pushed his claws into a fried mullet and *honoured* me and some others who were near him with the villainous morsel. It is thought an indispensable point of etiquette to devour such gifts, and most diverting it was to observe the grimaces, half concealed and half visible, which were made to gorge the savoury meat. A pinch of snuff from the box of the worshipful president causing one of his guests to sneeze, he burst into a loud and ridiculous laugh, in which he was joined by the attendants ;—it was judged a favourable omen * !

---

* The Ancient Greeks, it is well known, put great confidence in such auguries ;—so in the *Odyssey;*
　　　　　————" Telemachus then sneezed aloud ;
Constrained, his nostril echoed thro' the crowd.
The smiling queen the happy omen blest."
　　　　　　　　　　　　　　　BOOK XVII.

When the meal was concluded, we again adjourned to the divan; and fresh pipes, with excellent coffee, were presented to us. Moving toward the higher, that is the Aga's quarter of the mansion, we were furnished with pipes anew, and the *band* then made its appearance. It consisted of two violins, a sort of dulcimer, and a reed pipe, which last was played on by a Dervish. A second, who, by his dress and familiarity with the Aga, appeared of a superior rank, sat next, and assisted in the execution of a song, the worst, perhaps, that ever saluted mortal ears. Yet the whole presented a most curious scene. On the elevated and boarded part noticed before, occupying the whole divan, sat the officers of the Cambrian and Seringapatam; the Aga in one corner, with pipes three yards long, projecting from the jaw, and resting on the brass plate in the middle of the floor, while wreaths of thick smoke ascended to the roof. In front of this elevation sat the band, with the two Dervishes in their light-coloured sugar-loaf hats; and at their backs stood a huge crowd of turbaned attendants, filling up the whole space beyond, and looking with mute attention, and it may be, with internal ridicule, upon what was going forward. Would that I were a painter; or, would that I could *write* a painting!

After another pipe and glass of Champaigne, we departed in the same manner that we had arrived.

The Aga may be about fifty years of age, with a perfectly grey beard and sallow complexion *. A good-looking lad, of about six years, splendidly habited, and loaded with the usual quantity of arms, accompanied him. I should observe, that, till the Greek Revolution broke out, it was by no means customary to go so attired.

Monday, 17th Jan.—While I was reading this morning with my Greek master Kyriāca, a *Papas* entered the door of his apartment. It

---

* It is of him Lord Byron speaks in his Notes to the Second Canto of Childe Harold. "Suleyman Aga," says his lordship, " late Governor of Athens, and now of Thebes, was a *bon vivant*, and as social a being as ever sat crosslegged at a tray or a table. During the carnival, when our English party were masquerading, both himself and his successor were more happy to ' receive masks,' than any dowager in Grosvenor-square." It will be seen, that he still preserves his social character, as well as the means of supporting it.

was the Greek Epiphany; and he came according to custom, with a large sponge, a bottle of holy water, and a small cross. These he used in the following manner: He dipped the sponge into the holy water, and sprinkled the whole person of the Διδάσκαλος; he then presented to him the cross, which he reverently pressed to his lips. For this a piastre was to be paid; and as there are, at the present time, in Smyrna, upwards of twenty thousand Greeks of the national church, it may easily be seen what a rich harvest the Papas reap. Before the Revolution there were fifty thousand Greek inhabitants of Smyrna; and though the purchase of the water is optional, yet few omit a matter of such vital importance! The patriarchs are indeed said to derive the chief part of their income from the sale of this, and a holy chrism made annually, and dispersed wherever the influence of the religion prevails.

Towards the evening of this day, my very good friend Marsham (first-lieutenant of the Cambrian, and son of the Hon. and Rev. Jacob Marsham, Prebendary of Rochester, &c. &c.) performed such an act of devoted gallantry, as will go very near to render his name immortal,

as it deserves to be. The Greek slave of a
Turk, in Smyrna, took refuge from the barbarity of her master in the house of Mr. Fisher,
a Levant merchant. She was in a dreadful
plight when she came to him, bruised from
top to toe. The merchant compassionated her
situation, and harboured her till the arrival of
Captain Hamilton, to whom he immediately
applied for protection. Captain Hamilton,
always ready to assist the distressed, as hundreds of instances will prove, immediately
assented ; and they deliberated upon the best
steps to be taken in the affair. Our old friend
aforesaid was accordingly called in ; he has
ever been an acknowledged favourite of the
ladies, and has at all times a quick eye, a ready
hand, and a warm heart at their service. But
I shall make him blush—blush like the " Red
Book," which is for ever blushing, though I
guess not why exactly !—and scarce commo-
dities, we read, ought not to be lavished.
Waste not—want not, is an old and a very
sensible adage. To proceed : my friend sent
the dress of a midshipman to Mr. Fisher's
during the day ; and, at dusk, prepared his
pistols, put a keen edge upon his sword, and
15

a most intimidating fierceness into his look, being resolute to exterminate the whole town rather than fail in carrying off the black-eyed Grecian. It was the rape of a second Helen! and but for the inimitable prudence with which the affair was conducted, might have occasioned another ten years' war! But "thanks to the gods," as Addison makes Cato say, "my boy has done his duty;" he brought the fair lady in safety to the ship. And here, I may remark, by way of illustrating what I have said of the quickness of Mr. Marsham's eye, that the coat, waistcoat, and smallclothes which he selected, fitted her incomparably well;—not a fault could be found with them : so that I can, without hesitation, and with the utmost confidence, recommend him to any distressed damsel whatever, as the most perfect and peerless "Squire of Dames" that ever existed;—a chevalier, "sans peur et sans reproche."

This evening there was a ball at the French consul's, marked with all the characteristics of the preceding.

Tuesday, 18*th Jan.*—Sailed from Smyrna, and in the evening anchored off Vourla, in order to water the ships. The Seringapatam

sailed with us, under the orders of Captain
Hamilton, who is the senior officer of the station.   Vourla is distinguished by a number of
windmills on the heights; and various small
islands at their foot, give a beautiful and picturesque appearance to the bay.

Wednesday, 19th Jan.——Walked this morning, with my gun, across the hills; but started
no game.   The country here is more cultivated
than any part of Ionia that I have yet seen;
the olive and fig-tree are very abundant.   Returning by the shore, I discovered a creek,
which gave back a singularly fine echo. I also
picked up a few common shells.   The object
of most interest here, is a small island opposite
the ancient Clazomene, (now Vourla,) once
connected with the main land, and celebrated
for the mole, said to have been built by
Alexander the Great.   The foundations are
yet evident; and several ruins scattered over
the island, seem to bespeak a place of some
importance.   By the margin of a circular pit,
we found some specimens of a tesselated pavement; and I learn, from the chaplain of the
factory at Smyrna, that he and Lord St. Asaph
found considerable quantities, on excavating

the pit alluded to. In another part of the
island, there is a vaulted passage, supported
by a column, which seems now to serve the
purpose of a well. You descend by a flight
of steps, and a fig-tree flourishes upon the
summit. Beneath a niche in the remotest part
is a kind of sarcophagus, from which the lid
has been lifted, apparently, for examination.
Upon the beach I found many detached pieces
of Mosaic, of various colours and beauty. Some
of them resembled crystal, and others lapis
lazuli, &c. The echo, caused by the report of
a gun, reverberated exactly like thunder among
the hills.

Friday, 21st Jan.——Set sail for Thessalonica. About noon, the Cyrene, a twenty-gun
sloop of war, commanded by Captain Grace,
came in sight. She was telegraphed, and
ordered to join. It blew so hard during the
night, (though the wind was fair,) that we
carried away our main top-sails.

Saturday, 22d Jan.——This morning we came
in sight of the Olympian chain of mountains,
covered with snow. Ossa and Peleon (now
called Kissavo and Zagora) were distinctly
visible; Mount Athos, at intervals, might be

dimly perceived. The day was gloomy, and Olympus, which we passed, was enveloped in clouds; but as the sun struggled to break through, it cast, occasionally, on its hoary sides, many beautiful lights; and, before we anchored, gilded the whole chain with a shadowy magnificence.

We cast anchor off Thessalonica about six o'clock, P.M.

CHAPTER VI.

Sunday, 23d *Jan.*—Having performed divine service, we were put on shore in the cutter, and hastened to pay our respects to the English consul, Mr. Charnaud, whom we found the same obliging and friendly person that Dr. Clarke and other travellers have described. His son accompanied us in our researches. The Propylæum of the ancient Hippodrome, still survives; but it has been so much defaced by time and boyish wantonness, that its beauty is considerably impaired. It forms the side of a house, in which its columns are buried. Dr. Clarke speaks of five, but now there are only four. The figures are very much mutilated,— the same propensity (for it cannot be worse) appearing to exist here as in England. The lads hurl stones, and the Turks discharge their muskets, at the statues; so that their situation may easily be conjectured.

From the Hippodrome we proceeded to the Mosch of St. Demetrius. Dr. Clarke calls it the ancient Metropolitan Church: but this is a mistake; universal tradition ascribing it to the Mosch called Eska Djummee. Here, also, the Doctor, and Beaujour, whom he followed, are in error. They term it the Temple of the *Thermean Venus*. The truth is, it is a *Rotunda*, and built in imitation of the Pantheon. It has six large arched recesses in its sides; and the top has all the appearance of having been added when first used for a Christian church. The dome is in Mosaic, and nearly ruined. We picked up abundance of the coloured glass with which it was composed.

The *Eska Djummee*, therefore, the *Metropolitan Church*, and the *Rotunda*, are one and the same. There is in front of it what Dr. Clarke, speaking of the *latter*, calls a " magnificent marble béma, or pulpit," but it may rather be the ascent to one, since there are *steps* alone, winding, as we see them sometimes in the present day. The figures are in *basso-relievo*, armed cap-a-pie, and finely executed. But they cannot be very ancient; for the most conspicuous figure wears around

VOL. I.   N

his waist a sash, similar to those used by the
knights of the middle ages. *Here* also is the
fountain alluded to by Dr. Clarke, with " part
of an inscription, mentioning the name either
of *Cassander*, or of some citizen of CASSAN-
DRIA *," so that it is easy to identify the
place he means.

To return to the Mosch of St. Demetrius.——
It is in the form of a cross; and "on each side
is a double colonnade of pillars of the *Verde-
antico*, with *Ionic* capitals." So says Dr.
Clarke; but he adds, by way of note, " *Pococke*
says, these pillars are of white marble. It is
very possible, that under the circumstances of
our seeing the buildings of Salonica," [the
plague was then rife,] " an error of this kind
may have escaped our observation; but Beaujour has the same remark : ' La nef du milieu
est un beau vaisseau, soutenu par deux rangs
de colonnes de vert antique,' &c. Tableau du
Comm. de la Grece. Tom. I. p. 43 †." I have
not Beaujour by me to refer to; but as the
worthy consul declared, and as I have myself

* Clarke's Travels. Vol. VII. p. 453. 8vo. 1818.
† Ibid. p. 456.

already had sufficient opportunity to observe, Dr. Clarke has frequently made hasty and inaccurate remarks. There certainly *is* a double colonnade of pillars, but not of *Verde-antico*. Neither he nor Pococke is correct. The front rows have but *four pillars* of verde-antique, facing each other in the middle of the aisle : that row nearest the entrance, has six round pillars, of white marble, with the ornate capitals of Corinthian architecture, and three large pilasters or square shafts rising at proper distances between. Behind this colonnade are twelve small marble pillars, of the *Ionic order*. The opposite side of the aisle, besides the four verde-antique pillars already noticed, has five with Corinthian capitals, and two pilasters. Eleven small Ionic pillars are behind. To the right and left of the chancel, are four superb porphyry pillars, two on each side.

But of all Dr. Clarke's errors the following may perhaps be classed amongst the most remarkable. " The next day (Dec. 30th) Mr. Cripps accompanied Mr. Charnaud upon a shooting excursion into the country, to provide game for our journey ; the consul being very partial to this amusement, and glad to meet

with a companion as fond of it as himself;—
' We shall find plenty of game,' said he, ' but
you must promise to take away with you all
the *hares* that we may kill, for the *people of
this country* hold a dead hare in such detesta-
tion, that if I were to dress one for your dinner
I must take the skin off and roast it myself;
and the consequence would be, that none of
my servants would remain in the house where
it was flayed, or come into the room where it
was eaten.' This very ancient superstition was
before alluded to in this work; it was connected
with the worship of *Diana* among the *Greeks*.
But we find that fifteen centuries before the
Christian æra the *Israelites* were taught to
consider the *hare* as unclean; so that even to
touch it was an abomination. ' *The hare, because he cheweth the cud, but divideth not the
hoof, he is unclean unto you . . . . whosoever
toucheth the carcase shall be unclean* *.' ''

Of course I was desirous of gaining further
information relative to this curious story, especially since I remembered to have seen the
skins both of hares and rabbits constantly ex-

---

* Clarke's Travels, Vol. VII. p. 457, 8.

posed for sale by the Turks in Smyrna. Accordingly I applied to Mr. Charnaud, both younger and elder, and they both, particularly the latter, who was most concerned, assured me again and again, that there was not one particle of truth in the whole; on the contrary, the consul said that his cook would be very glad to dress them, since the skins are his perquisite; these he can sell to the furriers, who use them for a variety of purposes: and he added, that the Turks eat the flesh without the smallest hesitation.

What is here stated Mr. Charnaud afterwards repeated to several of our party: Mr. Strangways and I think Captain Hamilton and Captain Sotheby were both present, with many more.

The Mosch of St. Demetrius contains a fine Christian monument, with a Greek inscription relating to a female, an early convert to Christianity, which I have not time to copy:—the first line runs thus:

+ΑVΧΗΜΑΛΟΓΙΧΟCΓΕΤΟVΤΙJΗΓΛΛΗΝΛJΗΓΕΝΟVΟ

Various crosses are yet distinct upon the marble pavement, although the infidels have done

their utmost to obliterate every symbol of
Christianity.   Beneath this place is a subter-
raneous church now completely closed, in consequence, as it is said, of a man whose curiosity
led him to enter its dark vaults never having
been seen again.

The mosch next celebrated is that of St.
Sophia. On one of the towers is a stork's nest,
a bird held, it is well known, in universal veneration.   They arrive here early in March
and remain till August, but on the *fourth* of
that month precisely, (OLD STYLE!) every
bird takes its departure : not one is to be found
afterwards, nor is one missing till that very
day.   This peculiarity is no doubt amongst the
good reasons assigned by the Turks for the regard they shew them.

The Mosch of St. Sophia has nine pillars in
front, of which five are verde-antique and four
of red granite ; they contrast but poorly with
the white-washed Koran-scribbled walls of the
edifice.   Within are six pillars of verde-antique, three on each side : there is also a solid
pulpit of the same stone, which tradition has
denominated the pulpit of St. Paul.   From
hence he is said to have harangued the Thes-

salonians when he first attempted their conversion.   Idle as this tradition may be, the pulpit is of undoubted antiquity ; and both from the workmanship and quality of the materials which compose it, is deserving every attention.

A triumphal arch of Constantine at the southern extremity of Thessalonica is an admirable monument of the olden times ; but neither has it escaped the destroying hand of the Turk.   The arch itself has long been divested of the marble which enveloped the brickwork yet standing ; and the sculpture of one of the piers is surrounded by a baker's shop.   Nor is this all, the barbarians have knocked away the basso-relievos in order to introduce certain conveniences for their trade.   The other side is entirely boarded up, and if not already given to destruction, may on some future day afford an unexpected gratification.   Two compartments only are now visible, representing the triumph of CONSTANTINE (probably) in various situations.   In the higher compartment the victor is drawn in a triumphal car, accompanied by his guards, &c. and in the lower he is on horse-back ; over head an eagle hovers,

having a laurel crown in its talons, with which
it is just in the act of encircling the conqueror's
brows.   In our way hither from the Mosch of
St. Demetrius I discovered a square stone
about two feet high, on which the word
ΦΙΛΙΠΠΟΣ was inscribed.   We were. informed that a French consul attempted to dig
it up, but it was found buried too deep for the
purpose.   It is of singular shape, and unless it
has supported a statue I can form no conjecture
about it ; and it is unlikely to have done so if
it be of that height which the anecdote we
heard implies.

   At the northern quarter of the town is the
gate of the Vardar, which Dr. Clarke supposes
a triumphal arch of *Augustus :* a work far superior, he says, in point of taste to the other.
How this may be I know not ; the vault within
and without is overlaid with plaister by the
Turks, in two or three places it has given way ;
and passing the first archway of the vault on
the obverse side a section of a horse and man
may be discovered : under this arch I copied
the following inscription, which the younger
Mr. Charnaud believes cannot have been uncovered many years, yet Dr. Clarke speaks of

it cursorily as " containing the names of all the magistrates then in office."

ΠΟΛΕΙΤΑΡΧΟΥΝΤΩΝ·ΣΩΣΙΠΑΤΡΟΥ·ΤΟΥΚ/
ΠΑΤΡΑΣ·ΚΑΙ·ΛΟΥΚΙΟΥ·ΠΟΝΤΙΟΥ·ΣΕΚΟΥΝΔΟΥ
ΥΙΟΥ·ΑΥΛΟΥ·ΑΟ·ΥΙΟΥ·ΣΑΒΕΙΝΟΥ·ΔΗΜΗΤΡΙΟΥ·Τ
ΑΥΣΤΟΥ·ΔΗΜΗΤΡΙΟΥ·ΤΟΥ·ΝΕΙΚΟΠΘΛΕΟΣ·ΖΟ
ΤΟΥ·ΠΑΡΜΕΝΙΩΝΟΣ·ΤΟΥ·ΚΑΙΜΕΝΙΣΚΟΥ·ΓΑΙΟΥ·ΑΠΑΛΗΙΟΥ.
ΙΙΟΤ ΕΙΤΟΥ·ΤΑΜΙΟΥ·ΤΗΣ·ΠΟΛΕΟΣ·ΤΑΥΡΟΥ·ΤΟΥ·ΑΜΜΙΑΣ
ΤΟΥ·ΚΑΙΡΗΓΛΟΥ·ΓΥΜΝΑΣΙΑΡΧΟΥΝΤΟΣΤΑΥΡΟΤΟΥ ΤΑΥΡC
ΤΟΥΚΑΙΡΗΓΛΟΥ·

And a little to the right of the Vardar Gate is a fountain which has originally been an elegant soros of white marble, but which has not been noticed before : I find there an inscription in this form, erected by some one whose name I cannot decypher, " for his wife and himself, he being alive."

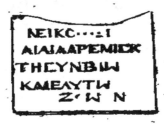

Wednesday, 26th Jan.—Mr. Charnaud obligingly accommodated me with the loan of a horse, and his son was good enough to attend me. I corrected the copies of some inscriptions which I had made, and from thence went to inspect a convent of dancing Dervishes outside the northern wall of the city. This is a curious place, but built much on the system of Catholic monasteries, that is, on one side the place of devotion and on the other little apartments for the Dervishes, containing a small divan, their sofa and bed. The building dedicated to the fantastic exercises of their religion is square, and painted both within and without. Within it is constructed like a *circus*, having a gallery above for the spectators; here they twirl in all the most ridiculous postures imaginable. *Cats* in immense numbers were running about the area; they feed and educate *sixty* of them in this convent alone (which is but small) and appear to consider them with the greatest veneration. Attached to the religious edifice is a tomb covered with a splendid cloth of gold, and crowned with the white turban of the Dervishes; it is called the tomb of the prophet, and I understand he has a similar mark of respect shewn him in every convent of the kind. It is surrounded by balconies, where the Dervishes walk.

10

Descending the hill we rode upon the level plain below it, and passed a khan, or inn, where certain travellers were reposing. These places are of the very worst description; all they can furnish you with, in general, is bread and a mat to sleep upon. Sometimes the only chamber is the stable ; and, to say truth, you might meet here worse companions than the horses. About a mile from the town is a sort of summer-house, to which the Pacha occasionally goes to divert himself, and enjoy the fresco of the sea. Half an hour's journey further is a high mound, which has all the appearance of a tumulus, and of which Dr. Clarke says, " that it may possibly cover the remains of those Thessalonians who fell in the battle fought here against Philip the Second ; no other instance having occurred likely to cause a *tumulus* of such magnitude so near to the walls of *Salonica*."

I returned to the ship with a promise from Mr. Charnaud, jun. to attend me, next day, to the dance of Dervishes, which is to take place at one o'clock P.M.

Thursday, 27th Jan.——There is a singular method of catching the red-legged partridges, common in this country, which I do not remember to have heard of before. The sportsman provides himself with a covering for his whole body composed of stripes of different kinds of the brightest cloth. He has a hole made in it for admitting his gun, and other holes for the eyes ; in which state he marches into the field. No sooner do the partridges perceive him, than impelled by this strange attraction, the whole covey run toward the cloth, and thus afford the sportsman an opportunity of murdering them at a blow !

Ibrahim, the present Pacha of Salonîca, is much esteemed here, and is universally spoken of as a humane man. We understand that he is nominated to a Pachalik of more importance, and will presently remove to it. Our arrival with three ships of war threw him into great consternation; he came down to the beach to make observations, and it is rumoured, gave orders for levying a competent force.

We hear that the Pacha of Egypt has sent his son with sixty men of war to Candia, and from twelve to fourteen thousand troops, in order to renew operations against the Greeks. But the Turks are so much in the habit of

11

crowding their ships with men as to render them unserviceable : in such cases the *Greek fire* must do infinite mischief. The Pacha's son is said to be a man of some talent, but not equal to his father.

Amongst other instances of the injudicious distribution of Bibles, by the BIBLE SOCIETY, which I find daily occurring, it was told me by Mr. Abbot, a Levant merchant in Salonica, that nearly four years ago, forty copies of the Bible, in different languages, had been sent to him from Malta ; of these he had, in vain, attempted to dispose of more than three. He also said, that though he had written several times to Malta, to point out the propriety of their being otherwise disposed of, no notice whatever had been taken of his suggestion. This, with various other anecdotes, which I doubt not I shall, from time to time, collect, should teach the Society that they may have mistaken the mode of accomplishing their object ; and that the flaming reports which they publish are not always borne out by facts. " In calculating the actual good done by the charitable contributions, which supply the funds of this benevolent association from year to year," says the Fifteenth Report of *the British and Foreign Bible Society,* page 212, " or the benefit derivable from the labours and exertions of the agents of the Society in any one year, the NUMBER OF VERSIONS AND COPIES OF THE HOLY SCRIPTURES, which are issued from the press in different languages, and forwarded to the places where they are meant to be distributed, MUST BE CONSIDERED A PRINCIPAL CRITERION AND MEASURE OF ESTIMATION. The committee have, therefore, great satisfaction in communicating, as part of the fruits of the past year, the completion of two distinct editions of the New Testament in three Asiatic languages, besides a small edition, in a fourth language, of the Gospel of St. Matthew." How fallacious a mode of arguing this is, I need not, after the facts already stated, trouble myself to shew ; but I must observe, that there seems not the smallest pretext for continuing the pernicious system of *penny collections* and *female associations,* if *such* be the use made of the supplies so raised.   If packages of books are sent off at random, left to casual distribution, and no enquiry made about them afterward, the money employed in these measures has been wasted, and the contributors cajoled!

Thursday Evening.—A singular anecdote, relative to Greek superstition, was told to me this evening. Three years after a body has been interred, the friends of the deceased make a procession to the place of its sepulchre, and examine the condition it is in. If the flesh be not decayed, or black, they imagine it to be the consequence of some enormous crime. They then have recourse to prayers and holy water, with which it is lavishly besprinkled, and again committed to the grave.

Friday, 28th Jan.—Sailed early for Scopeli, Captain Hamilton having received intelligence that several piratical ships had been cruising in this quarter, and had done considerable injury. We anchored in the evening off Cassandra.

Saturday, 29th Jan.—This day had nearly terminated most unhappily; and we have the utmost reason to be thankful for our escape from the dangerous extremity to which we were reduced. It blew violently, the ship running at a great rate. About noon we were off the little island of Skiatho, not more than a mile and a half from the coast, when we suddenly struck upon a rock, of which the charts take no notice, nor had any one on board the slightest knowledge of its existence. The crew, then on deck, were immediately summoned to the forecastle; and the position of the sails altered, in order to take every advantage of the wind. This method succeeded; she was brought off the rock, but the tiller-ropes had snapped, and the rudder, of course, would no longer obey the wheel. I was writing in my cabin at the time, and heard the ship's keel grating over the stone with no very pleasing sensations. Presently the whirl of the broken tiller-ropes threw down a quantity of glass in the after gun-room; and an impetuous rush from all the lower parts of the ship to the accommodation-ladder, plainly indicated the nature of the case. It was a striking scene that presented itself in the confused and hurried air of the men as they poured rapidly to their stations: the shouts of the officers, the rattling of the cordage, and the violent dashing of the sails against the creaking masts; add to this the roaring of the waves and the wind, through the very midst of all which,—

> " The shrill whistle of the boatswain's pipe
> Seemed as a whisper in the ear of death."

The gale continued freshening, and a thick haze obscured the distant mountains. The Seringapatam and Cyrene were telegraphed, and ordered to bear up toward the Gulf of Volo, (sinus Pelasgicus.) We anchored a little before three o'clock off Syrochoro, (an ancient town, which I am apprehensive we shall not see nearer at present,) and found twenty-eight inches of water in the hold. The pumps have been going continually ever since: our future destination is therefore doubtful.

Sunday, 30th Jan.—Still at anchor; but not permitted to go on shore. We are likely to return to Smyrna.

Monday, 31st Jan.—The weather has cleared up, and a beautiful though frosty morning makes amends for the dulness and disagreeableness of the preceding days. We are anchored in a kind of elliptical circle;—double chains of mountains towering above us on every side, and the farther and higher one mantled

in snow. To the east, are the ruins of Syrochoro, probably the ancient Dios, mentioned
by Homer and Strabo; but it seems unnoticed
altogether by modern travellers. At no great
distance from hence should be *Histiæa*, famous
for its vineyards; and *Cenæum*, a promontory
where Jupiter had a temple built by Hercules.
To the west of us, is a long ledge of white
rocks.

Contrary to expectation, soon after writing
the above, it was determined that we should
have communication with the shore. This had
been interdicted, from a primary intention of
returning immediately to Malta; and then
any thing of the sort would, of course, have
lengthened our quarantine there.

On landing, I immediately ascended a steep
hill, on which had been the acropolis of the
place. All that remains are walls, nearly extinct; but they have no appearance of any
great antiquity. The stones are cemented together; and broken buttresses or towers placed
at intervals around the line of wall, seem to
indicate a *Venetian* rather than a Grecian
fortress. It has been moated, and part of the
fosse yet exists. Two gateways are apparent,

the one on the north and the other to the
east, on which side, about fifty yards from the
wall, is a pit, of an elliptical form, nearly filled
up with shapeless stones and broken columns
of marble. Here, upon an overturned pedestal,
$26\frac{1}{2}$ feet high, and $21\frac{1}{2}$ broad, I discovered the
following inscription, which I take to be the
memorial of some amicable treaty between
persons whose names are no longer on record *.
It was written in very faint characters :—

ΔΕΞΙ1ΚΡΑΤΕΙ·
ΔΕΞΙΑΔΟΥ
ΕΙΛΙΤΗΙ

This was all, of any moment, that I discovered upon the acropolis. The pit is surrounded by young plane-trees. A Greek, who
was lounging here, informed me, that the
fortress had the name of ΩΡΑΙΟΝ, or the
Beautiful ; unless, indeed, the word was
ΟΡΙΟΝ, signifying the termination or boundary, as being close to the sea. The French
maps give the name of ORZO to a place nearer

* A friend suggests, that it signifies " to Dexicratinus,
the son of Dexiadus, a native of Elis." I leave it to the
reader.

the promontory of Cenæum; perhaps the ancient Histiæa. But it then becomes a question, whether the term be not misapplied? As I descended the hill, I observed a troop of Albanian soldiers, who, from the account given by the Greek above mentioned, were in pursuit of κλεφται, or robbers, and were patrolling up and down to that end. A small village had been ruined by the Turks in this place; amongst the rest, was a diminutive Grecian church, built in a cottage style, which had also fallen beneath their indiscriminating fury. In this place I discovered part of the rich entablature of a pillar; upon which was inscribed as follows:—

ΜΕΝΥΛΛΙ···ΤΙΜΑΣΙ··

Plutarch speaks of a *Menyllus* who attempted to prevail on Phocion to accept a sum of money; there is too little said, probably, to justify a supposition that it was the person alluded to. Here, also, I found a human skull, in a fine state of preservation. About half a mile further, surrounded by plane-trees, is a sort of dry pond; a low wall runs about it. I was informed that it had been a church, (ἐκκλησία);

but of that there was not the smallest trace.
Amongst the pile of stones forming the wall, I
found a broken one resting against a tree. I
seized upon it with eagerness, and bore it in
triumph to the ship. It was covered with the
writing which I have faithfully copied beneath.

```
                +
      ·····O IΛ∇Λ⅃······
    ·····WAN△⋎Ικ······
···ΘⱨⲤⴹⴹⲈⲠΟΙⱨⲤΛ κ
···ΓΕΡΟΝϽⲨΒΟⲨΛΟΜⱨΙΤΕΘ···
ΟⲨΤΟ
ⴺΛΟⲨΜΟⱾⲈΔΟⲨΝⴺΙⱨΡΟ⋎ΤΕϷ
ⲬⲰⲬⲤ2⌐ⴺⲬΙΤⱨⲔⲤⱭⴺΙⱾⴺ·Ϲ
ΘΡΑϜⱨⲤⱾⴺΝⱩⴺΕΙΝⱨⲤΓΕΝΘⲤⱯ····
ϷΟⲨϤΘⱨⲤΕⲨⲤΕϜΑⴺΟⲨΜⱨΝ
ⲤΕⱨⲤⴺⱨΡΕΤⱰⴺΝϜΟⲨΡΕⱰΑⳎΡⱯΝΕⲤΘⴺⴹ···
ΕΙⱨⱮΑⱰⱮⴺΙϜⴺ
··ⱨΙⲤΤⱯⲤϜΑΙΝⲨΝϜΑΤⴺⲬΕΒꞀΝⱬ
········ΘⱨΡⱯⲚ
·······     ·ⲠΕΝΘΟⲨΤΑΚ⌀ϚⴺΓϜ···
········    ·ⴺⱰⴹΑΘΟⱨⱨϜ·······
··········    ⅂ΟΝ·············
```

The contractions, or rather the *conjunctions*
of many of the letters might, perhaps, be considered an argument against the *very* ancient
date of the inscription. And taking this idea
as a guide, it would not be fixed earlier in all
probability than the lower empire. But several
of the letters undoubtedly bear the shape of

the earliest age: such, for instance, is the
theta Θ, sigma C, although it occurs in inscriptions of later times,—alpha A, joined in
the fourteenth line to lambda $\mathsf{\lambda}$, thus, $\mathsf{A\lambda}$, and
Y, which resembles the ancient gamma.

It is curious to observe the word $\Theta\mathsf{H}\mathsf{C}\mathsf{E}\mathsf{Y}\mathsf{C}$,
(THESEUS,) distinctly legible in the ninth line;
but I pretend not to explain its meaning.

$$\Theta\rho\acute{\alpha}\kappa\eta\varsigma\ \mu\grave{\epsilon}\nu\ \kappa\lambda\epsilon\acute{\iota}\nu\eta\varsigma\ \cdot\ .\ .\ .\ .$$
$$.\ .\ .\ .\ .\ \Theta\acute{\eta}\sigma\epsilon\upsilon\varsigma\ \acute{\epsilon}\kappa\alpha\lambda\upsilon\tilde{\upsilon}\mu\eta\nu$$

is nearly as much as I can decypher.

While we were out upon our excursion, the
Cyrene had spoke with an Ionian brig, of which
she distinguished two pirates in chase.   The
brig was afterwards boarded; and, in answer
to certain queries, stated, that several piratical
vessels were cruising up the gulf.   This intelligence being communicated to Capt. Hamilton,
measures were immediately taken; and, on our
return, we found them busy in manning and
arming the boats.   Four were sent from each
ship; that is, from the Cambrian and Seringapatam,—the Cyrene being absent.   They were
put under the command of Lieut. Marsham,
who rowed on before the rest, with orders to
persuade the pirates, if possible, to submit
11

themselves to examination; and for that purpose to bring up their vessels to the station of our ships. But he was strictly enjoined to forbear all attack, unless every other alternative was rejected, and no other mode offered itself of accomplishing the object of his mission.

They left the ships at four o'clock, P.M. and returned about one in the morning, with two small vessels and seventeen of their crews; some of whom were dangerously wounded. Unhappily four of our own men were killed in the fray; and sixteen out of both ships severely hurt. Lieut. Worsfall, of the Seringapatam, received three wounds in the breast, which but for the thickness of his coat, and the slanting direction which the balls had taken, must have proved fatal. As it happened, however, they went no further than the skin. In fact, the pirates fought desperately to a man; and such was their resolution, that, in the last violent effort to escape, having discharged their pieces, they dashed them furiously at the assailants, and leapt headlong into the water.——Something of the spirit of old Greece, manifested in a bad cause, seemed forcibly to prevail here! Their Captain died, after the conflict, in his way to the ships, of a wound from a pistol ball, which had penetrated the breast, and with several sabre-wounds in the lower part of his body. He was stretched out, for a short time, upon the quarter-deck, covered with a flag,—a horrible and an awful sight : his face, which must have been handsome, was shockingly smeared with blood : and his long black hair, clotted and spread in disorder around him, gave a singular wildness to his appearance, as seen by a bright moon on the quarter-deck of a man of war. His mouth, the upper lip of which had long mustachios, was stiff with gore, and his eyes were unclosed : adding yet more strongly to the savageness of feature, which his last bold act contributed to impress upon him. The dark eye of his country gleamed fiercely even in death : but it was said, that he died uttering "*Christiano, Christiano,*"—a characteristic, or at least *Catholic* termination of an unlawful career !

Following up his instruction to the letter, Mr. Marsham first proceeded, with his own boat, only in search of the pirates; and, having fallen in with them, explained, through an interpreter, the necessity of their complying with

the wishes of the English commodore. He
assured them of safety, provided they acquiesced; and endeavoured, by maintaining an
easy unconstrained tone, to obviate the irri-
tation, or apprehension, perhaps, which their
manner throughout had indicated, as well as
to afford time for the hindmost boats to come
up. All that he could say proving ineffectual,
he gave them to understand that they must
expect the worst; and pushed off to meet his
companions. It was now night; and though
the moon had arisen in great splendour, yet
the shadow of the lofty mountains, beneath
which they rowed, obscuring the track of the
pirates, involved our boats in doubt and perplexity. At this period they fell in with a
small trading vessel, called, technically, a
Bonebard, who directed them to the probable
haunts of the desperadoes; and who, at the
same time, requested for themselves a convoy
down the gulf. The search was then sedulously
pursued; and about nine o'clock they distinguished the two vessels, which they afterwards
took, off Cape Lethada, the ancient CENÆUM.

It is probable that the pirates had no idea
of so large a force being at hand. On Lieut.

Marsham's first approach alone, their intentions seemed decidedly hostile; and they several times attempted to bring a large gun, placed at the bow of their vessel, to bear upon the boat. This he, of course, avoided; but when the sound of oars nearing them was again heard, the belief of the officers very generally was, that the pirates looked only for the return of the same boat, which they were pre-determined to attack. For no sooner had the leading boat come within shot, than a volley of musketry, fired from the piratical vessels, struck seven of our men: but surely, if they had been aware of the approach of eight well-armed boats, they would rather have preferred standing rigidly upon the defensive. Their proceeding, however, was the signal for a quick and destructive fire. Many of the Greeks, after a desperate and well-contested struggle of twenty minutes, plunged into the water: fifteen were afterwards thrown overboard dead; and the remainder, brought prisoners to the ship. There certainly could not have been less than forty men, crowded into two puny vessels of not more than twenty tons burden. Amongst those who were captured, was a boy of twelve or thirteen years of age. During the conflict, he had crept to the bottom of the boat; and it was with the utmost difficulty that he could be drawn forth. With less manliness than his age promised, he screamed most piteously. It is a curious fact, that one of the prisoners resembles the *ci-devant Governor of Scio* most strikingly. This was noticed by many beside myself.

Throughout the whole of the affair, the greatest credit is reflected upon the officers who conducted it. As far as my own knowledge goes, I should say, that than Mr. Marsham, the first, and Mr. Smart, the fourth, Lieutenant, of the Cambrian, there could not have been officers selected more fitted for the occasion, or for any other. Spirit, judgment, and humanity, are alike their characteristics, as they are those of the whole British navy. What I say of one I say of all.

Tuesday, 1st Feb.——The prisoners who had been taken yesterday, were sent to the Cyrene, to be conducted to Scopeli, and delivered up to the government. One of these was a PAPAS. From papers found upon them, added to the confession of one of the party, no doubt can exist of their piratical pursuits. Their vessels have been burnt, after undergoing a minute inspection, and the contents disposed of on board our own ships. The large gun mentioned before, was found crammed up to the top with nails, round stones, and other offensive materials of the same nature. It had been fired several times the preceding day, but apparently without effect. In the belt of the deceased chief, a quantity of silver and gold was discovered, not amounting to more than a few pounds, and bearing principally the form of amulets. The greater part of their weapons the pirates themselves had thrown overboard, when further resistance was fruitless.

The dead bodies of our men were deposited in the sea, with military honours. Two boats were manned; in one lay the corpses, and in the other were the marines under arms. I accompanied the former boat, with the first lieutenant, about a cable's length from the ship; the band on deck playing solemn music. The funeral service was read, and the waters closed over them. They had yesterday gone forth breathing—living men; full of hope and exultation. They laughed with the laughers;

and returned the coarse jest of their companions with noisy thoughtless glee. Before the ensuing dawn, they were dead: a piece of canvas, bound tightly to the body, was their winding-sheet—the echo of musketry their requiem—and the wave, as it parted to receive them into its bosom, poured forth almost the last tribute to their memory! No matter; *that*

> " ἰερὸν ὕπνον
> Κοιμᾶται *,"

and the deepest and the truest lamentation, is useful only as it affects the mind and heart and subsequent conduct of the living. "Mais la mort," says a Frenchman, whose name I forget, " la mort, n'est autre chose, que le regret des vivans; si nous ne la regrettons pas, il n'est pas mort." The idea is all over *French*.

Wednesday, 2d Feb.——Weighed anchor at an early hour. The Seringapatam hailed another boat which had suffered from the depredations of the pirates. About ten o'clock we discovered five small *Latine* vessels sailing

* Callimachus.

close under the coast of Thessaly, immediately at the entrance of the Gulf of Volo.
Supposing them a part of the piratical cruizers
they were fired at, for the purpose of being
brought too : they were not, however, within
shot.   It was a beautiful morning with light
winds which just served to ripple the surface of
the water.   The *Latines* furled their sails, put
back, and pulled into a narrow creek, where
they were safe for the time from molestation :
they then climbed the rocks to watch our motions.   As the object of Captain Hamilton was
only to ascertain who and what they were, he
wished to try every conciliating measure before
he resorted to any thing harsh.   With this
view he despatched one of the wounded prisoners who remained, with a flag of truce, and
a request that some of their leaders would
come on board his ship.   In the mean time
preparations were made for a refusal.   The
marines were called up and drilled ; ball cart-
ridges brought out, with pistols, muskets and
cutlasses for the whole crew.   It certainly was
an animating scene ; the snapping of flints was
perpetual, and the bustling, not to say *joyous*,
air of the younger officers, was strong evidence

how vividly they felt the power of what was going forward.

On the return of the boat, after leaving our ambassador in the hands of his countrymen, we had a picturesque account of their proceedings. They approached without seeing a man, but as soon as they had landed the prisoner and retired, a whistle was heard, and immediately upwards of a hundred men sprung from beneath the bushes of the rocks. The incident in Sir W. Scott's " *Lady of the Lake*," that, namely, of Roderic Dhu and his clansmen instantly recurred ! Allowing a sufficient time for consultation our boat was despatched a second time, and returned with four or five Greeks, for whose safety our first lieutenant, perhaps unwisely, had chosen to remain as a hostage; however, he was treated with every civility.

The account given by these people was, that they were gun-boats belonging to a small Greek squadron, consisting of two brigs, a schooner, and what is called a *mystico*, (which is something resembling a very small schooner) cruising on the opposite side of the gulf. It seems that twelve Turkish vessels are now in

Volo, and that the Greeks have fitted out this armament with a design to intercept and burn the fleet of their enemy. The Cyrene, however, had met with the gun-boats last evening, and had fired at them for a considerable time. From all these circumstances they concluded that we were Turkish men of war, and our steady pursuit confirmed them in the idea. In conclusion, they agreed to accompany us to the station of the larger vessels from which they had been detached.

The sun set even more magnificently than usual. On one side was the coast of Thessaly, bending round us like a bow, with Mount Parnassus towering in the distance; on the other side was the Island of Negropont; the Islands of Scopeli, Skiatho, and Pondico-nisi to the east.

Only one of the Greek vessels having issued from the creek, according to the agreement, our boats were again manned and armed, and with Captain Hamilton himself at their head, proceeded to act as occasion might dictate. First, however, a boat set forth with a flag of truce, and found the Greeks all on the alert, and stationed amongst the bushes, with their musquets ready for the action, which they seemed to think inevitable. A parley now ensued, which lasted till sun-set, when they were persuaded to come along side of our ship: but this object, though advised and wished by their leaders, was effected with difficulty, and Captain Hamilton, to quiet apprehensions which appeared to increase rather than abate, went singly into one of their boats, standing as calmly when exposed to the range of their musquets as he would have done upon the deck of his own ship. By this time a boat belonging to the Greek brig of war, despatched by her commander, arrived at the creek, and this, no doubt, contributed a good deal to dissipate the alarms occasioned (as we found) by the invincible belief of our being Turkish or *Austrian* ships. It seems that the latter have, in several recent instances, betrayed them into the hands of their foes. I have heard it stated, on good authority, that an Austrian admiral, having invited a Greek primate on board his ship, so far forgot himself and his station as to lift up his hand and knock down the poor Greek on the quarter-deck ! Surely their fears were not altogether unreasonable !

The place to which we pursued the gun-boats is not far from Trichiri; had we therefore, under supposition of their being pirates, pointed our guns so as to have blown up their vessels, they must, in all probability, have fallen a prey to the Turks. As to those we destroyed two days before, they acknowledged that they were pirates, and seemed well pleased at the result of the contest. Captain Hamilton, with his usual kindness, presented them with two bags of bread and half a dozen bottles of rum.

Trichiri is in possession of the Turks. A strange fact with relation to this place is, that its absolute defence rests upon the exertions and loyalty of one hundred and fifty GREEKS of Scopeli and the neighbourhood, who are in the pay of the Turks. There are also three hundred of them at Negropont. Contrary to the usual practice, they are suffered to carry arms, and are kept under, more by the sequins than by the fear of their masters. What would the *three hundred of Thermopylæ* have thought and done in a like situation ? But these men, as I was informed by a Greek from the brig of war, chiefly compose the bands of pirates who infest Scopeli; and part of whom we destroyed (which is curious!) not more than ten miles from the celebrated pass just alluded to.

Thursday, 3d Feb.——Calm all the morning. At noon we passed Skyropouli, anciently *Scyros*, the scene of the early youth of Achilles, and of his discovery in the disguise of a girl by the dexterous management of Ulysses. Mount Athos was upon our left.

CHAPTER VII.

SATURDAY, *5th Feb.*——Arrived at Smyrna. This morning one of the sailors wounded in the contest with the pirates died; and the Greek prisoners who had been sent to Scopeli were returned, with a request from the government that they might be hung. Parted company with the Seringapatam. She has been ordered to Milo.

With regard to the actual situation of the Greeks, the " *English public*" have been considerably misinformed. The Papers are filled with falsehoods. We received the " Liverpool Courier" to-day, by the kindness of the captain of a merchantman, bearing date the 20th December. Lord Gordon and a " gallant company" are here said to have arrived at Napoli, with forty stands of colours wrought by the fair hands of the ladies of Edinburgh. We were in that place (Napoli) for several days, from the 25th of Dec. and I need not add, that the report is totally unfounded. The Greeks are stated to have taken several ships of the line from the Turks——this also is false: they have, since the commencement of the Revolution, *burnt* two or three, but they do not possess, perhaps, in their whole navy, a larger vessel than a brig of two hundred tons at the *very utmost.* Those which we have met with hitherto have not exceeded thirty or forty tons. The truth is, they are unable to build and equip ships of any magnitude, and they have not funds sufficient to purchase them. With their small vessels they cruise up and down the islands, and principally by means of *fire,* effect the destruction of the larger ships of the enemy. But then the Turks are so incorrigibly supine, that though their actual losses are, in comparison with their resources, very trifling; yet they suffer more by this desultory mode of warfare than by undergoing positive defeats. The subjects of the Porte already begin to murmur; and reports are abroad that the present sultan will be dethroned ere long, and his son, a lad of about nine years old, set up in his place. In fact,

the janizaries are said to be in a state of actual
rebellion, owing to the measures of *depression*
which the reigning sovereign has long adopted.
He would fain weaken their influence, and
when a contest of this kind is carried on between parties so constituted, it is not difficult
to foresee the result.

The Greeks, I am quite clear, have all the
qualities necessary for making them redoubted
warriors : patience, perseverance, and a high
determined valour are their characteristics ;
so far as I have seen, there has been no reason
to charge them with bad faith.   But I have as
yet seen little ; and their very acuteness, which
is universally admitted, argues, I fear, (when
considered with reference to their depressed
and persecuted condition) a propensity to exert
it in a bad cause as well as in a good one.   I
have heard numberless anecdotes of their obstinacy, treachery, and petty trickery ; but of
these I do not credit half ; and of the rest, I
think that there may perhaps be many circumstances, concealed or not understood, which
might palliate and almost justify the facts,
which *primâ facie* are deserving of the harshest
denomination.   It is extremely difficult where

10

we now are to obtain accurate information of what is going forward ; the Greeks themselves exaggerate their successes, and the Turks falsify them *in toto.*   But unquestionably the balance of fortune is on the side of the former ; and I verily believe that their own misconduct alone can prevent the ultimate attainment of their liberties.

Sunday, 6th Feb.—Four Greeks of Smyrna having attempted an escape on board an Ionian vessel, were retaken by the Turks and put to death.   It is customary for the executioner here to use a long and sharp sword in the performance of his office, at which he is sufficiently dexterous, but in the present case (for what reason is not apparent) an ataghan had been employed.   The men knelt down upon the quay near the Pacha's house, with bared necks, and heads drooped for the stroke of death.   In the number of these unhappy victims to Turkish cruelty was an old man ; he also was placed in the manner I have mentioned, but instead of taking off the head, the ataghan fell upon the hinder part of it, sinking deep into the skull, and he was actually struck SEVEN times before the murder could be completed. In the mean while the place re-echoed with his cries and groans; and when one of the English residents in Smyrna, attracted by the noise, approached the spot, the heads were thrown upon a heap, and the trunks spouted forth a flood of gore! Such are the scenes to which the Turkish government accustoms its subjects; and such are the facts at which, while humanity shudders, the Mussulman only exults!

The dead body of the sailor was interred this afternoon in the burial-ground of the Factory, with military honors: the marines, with their arms reversed, preceded by the band playing the dead march in Saul, and followed by the officers and seamen, accompanied the body through the streets of Smyrna :——the day was rainy.

Monday, 7th Feb.——We were at a ball this evening given by an American merchant——the agent of the American government. The Turks refuse to acknowledge the independence of the Americans, and will not allow them a *consul* in the place. Suleiman Aga, (our old friend) was present at the ball, and seemed vastly entertained with what he saw. It is understood that he applied for an admission to the balls of the Casino, but that it was not thought proper to assent to his request. The reason assigned is, that a former Pacha who was admitted to these assemblies (he has since lost his head!) behaved himself with great indecorum, not only smoking and ejecting his *saliva* upon the dresses of the damsels, but even accosting them in improper language. They fear, therefore, that the admission of Suleiman would become a bad precedent; and that the future would be marked with consequences prejudicial alike to themselves and their assemblies. This, it must be owned, is a good reason enough; but others have said, that some little jealousy of the French, &c. arising from the civilities shewn by the Aga to Englishmen, has prompted the refusal. I have nothing to say upon the point : either or both of the causes may have had their weight. Suleiman indeed avers, that were he ten years younger he would make a trip to England; and a superb double-barrelled " MANTON" which he has procured, testifies that English manufactures have no less charms for him than English society.

Wednesday, 9th Feb.——Strolled with Mr. Arundell, whose kindness and antiquarian research keep equal pace with his many other good qualities, to the Castle of Smyrna on Mount Pagus, in pursuit of relics. Amongst the loose stones of the Amphitheatre I picked up a small one, almost triangular in shape, and of about four inches and a half long, with the following inscription——too abrupt, I fear, to lead to any thing determinate.

I found a second, but it was even less perfect than the one I have copied. Mr. Arundell was more fortunate, and he will, I hope, before long give the result of his accumulated researches to the public.

On our return we were overtaken by two Turks, who seemed mightily inquisitive as to the nature of our pursuits. One of them had a most ferocious aspect, and his conduct altogether was assuming and impudent. As we descended the Mount one gave the other a push, and out flew their *ataghans*—a prospect with which we were little fascinated. It seemed done for the purpose of intimidation; and immediately afterwards one of them approached me and signified by signs that my *gloves* had taken his fancy; however I had no fancy to part with them, and I have made a memorandum never to ascend Mount Pagus again without the accompaniment of a brace of pistols.

Thursday, 10th Feb.——I was present to-day, at the funeral of a Greek boy—it was curious and interesting. The friends and relations of the deceased assemble at a certain hour, and seat themselves on the divan or on chairs around the corpse, which is placed in the centre of the room, arrayed in splendid funeral habiliments, and with its head turned toward the east; they then kiss its cold and pallid cheeks, and utter many lamentations, all of which are addressed to the body. The mother, or, if the deceased be a married man, his wife, takes the principal share in the ceremony, weeping, beating her breast, and talking to it, sometimes with gentle reproaches, as if it could actually hear and understand all that was said *. When this has been acted sufficiently, the corpse is deposited on a kind of bier, and preceded by a number of *papas*, walking two and two, and ringing in a loud nasal tone perpetual changes upon the following words:

Ἅγιος ὁ θεὸς, ἅγιος ἰσχυρὸς, ἅγιος ἀθάνατος ἐλέησον ἡμᾶς,

which signify " Holy God, holy strong One, holy Immortal, pity us ;" and are descriptive of the three persons of the Trinity. Thus they enter the church, where the archbishop (if the

---

* See the translated Gesta Romanorum, Vol. I. page 73, 4. and see also the Hero and Leander of Musæus. Thus Chapman—

" And as when funeral dames watch a dead corse
Weeping about it ; telling with remorse
What pains he felt, how long in pain he lay,
How little food he ate, what he would say :
And then mix mournful tales of others' deaths,
Smothering themselves in clouds of their own breaths.
At length, one cheering other, calls for wine :
The golden bowl drinks tears from out their eyne,
As they drink wine from it ; and round it goes,
Each helping other to relieve their woes."

deceased be of consequence, and rich enough
to command the services of so great a man !)
is seated on a gilded throne attached to a
pillar in the centre aisle. They approach and
place the body before him, exclaiming at the
same time, Εἰς πολλὰ, ἔτη δεσπότα—" May
you live many years, Lord." Δεσπότης is
used only in addressing the archbishop. Two
lights are burnt at the head and two at the
feet of an adult, but a child has only one at
the foot. They then recommence singing
certain passages from the Psalms; and small
waxen tapers are given to every person of respectable appearance present. The tapers are
lighted and clouds of frankincense (supposed
to carry in their ascent the prayers of the
afflicted relatives to heaven!) are scattered
lavishly about. After this the lights are ex-
tinguished, and such of the crowd as are connected with the deceased rush forward to take
the last kiss : they press their lips eagerly to
the cheeks, breast, &c. but principally to the
cheek. The body is then carried to the grave ;
divested in a rude and disgusting manner of
the decorations with which it had come forth,
and moistened with a quantity of oil, or more

frequently with water upon which a small portion of oil floats. This is done by the priest, accompanied with a short prayer, from a belief that the dissolution of the body would not otherwise take place.

The Greeks bury their dead within ten hours after the vital spark appears to be extinct. If this happen in the morning they are buried before night, if toward evening they watch the corpse till daylight, and then hasten the interment. This singular precipitation has frequently been followed by *revivals*, which terminate in an excruciating and lingering death. The places of sepulture are a kind of small pits, capable of containing many human bodies when they are extended one above the other at full length. The pits are paved, partitioned from each other by a slight brickwork, and covered with a flat stone, upon which the names of the dead and figures symbolical of their trade or profession are engraved *. Into this, without coffin, and with scarce a shroud, the corpse is put; so that the horrible situation

* This is usual also upon the tomb-stones of the Jews : for instance, a pen and ink-stand denotes a scribe; a pair of scissors a tailor, &c. &c.

of one awakening from a trance may easily be
imagined. These depositaries just admit air
enough to prolong suffering, and however
forcible be his cries they serve only to awake
the apprehensions of the living, without affording succour to the dying and despairing
wretch. The layman hears the utterance of
his agony, and instantaneously drops upon his
knees ; the *papas* hears it, and has recourse to
prayers and fumigations, but human aid is
hopeless. The truth indeed is, that they conceive certain evil spirits called VROUCOLOCHAS
have seized upon the dead, and that *they* produce the terror-striking shrieks which issue
from the subterranean recesses. A singular
story relating to these spirits is told by M.
Tournefort, and as the book is scarce, and the
anecdote (marvellous though it be) from what
I have both seen and heard, likely to be fact,
I shall give it without curtailment.

" The man, whose story we are going to
relate, was a peasant of Mycone, naturally ill-
natured and quarrelsome. This is a circumstance to be taken notice of in such cases. He
was murdered in the fields, nobody knew how,
nor by whom. Two days after his being buried

in a chapel in the town, it was noised about
that he was seen to walk in the night with
great haste, that he tumbled about people's
goods, put out their lamps, griped them behind, and a thousand other monkey tricks. At
first the story was received with laughter; but
the thing was looked upon to be serious when
the better sort of people began to complain of
it: the papas themselves giving credit to the
fact, and no doubt had their reasons for so
doing: masses must be said to be sure, but for
all this the peasant drove his old trade, and
heeded nothing they could do. After divers
meetings of the chief people of the city, of
priests and monks, it was gravely concluded
that 'twas necessary, in consequence of some
musty ceremonial, to wait till nine days after
the interment should be expired.

" On the tenth day they said one mass in
the chapel where the body was laid in order
to drive out the demon which they imagined
was got into it. After mass they took up the
body, and got every thing ready for pulling
out its heart: the butcher of the town, an old
clumsy fellow, first opens the belly instead of
the breast, he groped a long while among the

entrails, but could not find what he looked
for; at last somebody told him he should cut
up the diaphragm.   The heart was pulled out
to the admiration of all the spectators.   In the
mean time the corpse stunk so abominably
that they were obliged to burn frankincense,
but the smoke mixing with the exhalations
from the carcase increased the offensive smell,
and began to muddle the poor people's peri-
cranies.   Their imagination, struck with the
spectacle before them, grew full of visions :
it came into their noddles that a thick smoke
arose out of the body; we durst not say 'twas
the smoke of the incense.   They were incessantly bawling out *Vroucolacas* * in the chapel
and place before it ; this is the name they give
to these pretended *Redivivi*.   The noise bel-
lowed through the streets, and it seemed to be
a name invented on purpose to rend the roof of
the chapel.   Several there present averred that

* " Vroucolacas, Βρουκόλακος καὶ Βρουκόλακας, καὶ Βρουκο-
λάκας. Βρουκόλακας, a spectre consisting of a dead body
and a demon.   Some think that Βρουκολακυς signifies a
stinking carcase denied Christian burial.   Βρούκος and
Βουρκος, that nasty stinking slime which subsides at the
bottom of old ditches ; for Λακος signifies a *ditch*."

the wretch's blood was extremely red; the
butcher swore the body was still warm, whence
they concluded that the deceased was a very
ill man for not being thoroughly dead, or in
plain terms, for suffering himself to be re-ani-
mated by *Old Nick,* which is the notion they
have of a *Vroucolacas.* They then roared out
that name in a stupendous manner. Just at
the time came in a flock of people, loudly pro-
testing they plainly perceived the body was not
grown stiff when it was carried from the fields
to church to be buried, and that consequently
it was a true *Vroucolacas;* which word was
still the burden of the song.

"I dont doubt they would have sworn it
did not stink had not we been there; so mazed
were the poor people with this disaster, and so
infatuated with their notion of the dead's being
reanimated. As for us, who were got as close
to the corpse as we could, that we might be
more exact in our observations, we were almost
poisoned with the intolerable smell that issued
from it. When they asked us what we thought
of this body, we told them we believed it to be
very thoroughly dead; but as we were willing
to cure, or at least not to exasperate their pre-

judiced imaginations, we represented to them that it was no wonder the butcher should feel a little warmth when he groped among entrails that were then rotting; that it was no extraordinary thing for it to emit fumes, since dung turned up will do the same; that as for the pretended redness of the blood, it still appeared by the butcher's hands, to be nothing but a very stinking nasty smear.

" After all our reasons they were of opinion it would be the wisest course to burn the dead man's heart on the sea-shore: but this execution did not make him a bit more tractable; he went on with his racket more furiously than ever; he was accused of beating folks in the night, breaking down doors, and even roofs of houses, clattering windows, tearing clothes, emptying bottles and vessels. 'Twas the most thirsty devil! I believe he did not spare any body but the consul, in whose house we lodged. Nothing could be more miserable than the condition of this island; all the inhabitants seemed frightened out of their senses. The wisest among them were stricken like the rest. 'Twas an epidemical disease of the brain, as

dangerous and infectious as the madness of
dogs. Whole families quitted their houses,
and brought their tent-beds from the farthest
parts of the town into the public places, there
to spend the night. They were every instant
complaining of some new insult ; nothing was
to be heard but sighs and groans at the approach of night. The better sort of people retired into the country.

" When the prepossession was so general we
thought it our best way to hold our tongues.
Had we opposed it we had not only been accounted ridiculous blockheads, but Atheists and
infidels. How was it possible to stand against
the madness of a whole people? Those that believed we doubted the truth of the fact came and
upbraided us with our incredulity, and strove
to prove that there were such things as *Vrou-
colacasses* by citations out of the *Buckler of
Faith*, (Τάργα τῆς Ρωμαικῆς πίστεως) written
by F. Rechard, a Jesuit missionary. He was
a *Latin*, say they, and consequently you ought
to give him credit. We should have got nothing by denying the justness of the consequence : it was as good as a comedy to us every

morning to hear the new follies committed by
this night-bird; they charged him with being
guilty of the most abominable sins.

"Some citizens that were most zealous for
the good of the public, fancied they had been
deficient in the most material part of the ceremony. They were of opinion that they had
been wrong in saying mass before they had
pulled out the wretch's heart: had we taken
this precaution, quoth they, we had bet the
devil as sure as a gun; he would have been
hanged before he would ever have come there
again. Whereas, saying mass first, the cun-
ning dog fled for it a while, and came back
again when the danger was over.

"Notwithstanding these wise reflections,
they remained in as much perplexity as they
were the first day. They meet night and
morning, they debate, they make processions
three days and three nights, they oblige the
papas to fast: you might see them running
from house to house, holy-water brush in hand,
sprinkling it all about, and washing the doors
with it; nay, they poured it into the mouth of
the poor *Vroucolacas.*

"We so often repeated it to the magistrates

(Ἐπιτρόποι) of the town, that in *Christendom* we should keep the strictest watch a-nights upon such an occasion, to observe what was done, that at last they caught a few vagabonds who undoubtedly had a hand in these disorders; but, either they were not the chief ringleaders, or else they were released too soon, for two days afterwards, to make themselves amends for the Lent they had kept in prison, they fell foul again upon the wine-tubs of those who were such fools as to leave their houses empty in the night. So that the people were forced to betake themselves again to their prayers.

" One day, as they were hard at this work, after having stuck I know not how many naked swords over the grave of this corpse, which they took up three or four times a day, for any man's whim, an Albaneze, that happened to be at *Mycone*, took upon him to say, with a voice of authority, that it was to the last degree ridiculous to make use of the swords of Christians in a case like this. Can you not conceive, blind as ye are, says he, that the handles of these swords being made like a cross, hinder the devil from coming out of the body? why do you not rather take the Turkish sabres? The advice of this learned man had no effect: the *Vroucolacas* was incorrigible; and all the inhabitants were in a strange consternation. They knew not now what saint to call upon, when of a sudden, with one voice, as if they had given each other the hint, they fell to bawling out all through the city, that it was intolerable to wait any longer,—that the only way left was to burn the *Vroucolacas* entire; that after so doing, let the devil lurk in it if he could; that it was better to have recourse to this extremity, than to have the island totally deserted. And indeed whole families began to pack up in order to retire to Syra or Tinos. The magistrates therefore ordered the *Vroucolacas* to be carried to the point of the Island of St. George, where they prepared a great pile, with pitch and tar, for fear the wood, as dry as it was, should not burn fast enough of itself. What they had before left of this miserable carcase, was thrown into this fire, and consumed presently: 'twas on the first of January, 1701. We saw the flame as we returned from Delos; it might justly be called a bonfire of joy, since after this no more complaints were heard against the *Vroucolacas ;* they said that the devil had now met with his match, and some ballads were made to turn him to ridicule."

This strange superstition, Tournefort, all bigotted as he is, very properly ridicules ; but honestly speaking, the Greeks are to the full, with a few exceptions indeed, as much prepossessed with the feeling as they were a century ago. The Greek Papas are ignorant in the extreme ; and struggle hard to keep their flock in the same pitiable condition. It is a remarkable circumstance, that one of those persons, in Smyrna, bears the most perfect resemblance to the portrait of our Saviour, as painted by the masterly hand of Carlo Dolce. He wears his hair parted in front, and hanging to a considerable length down his shoulders. Strange to say, he is nearly an idiot. The likeness is undoubted, and has struck numbers ; amongst the rest, my friend Arundell is a host of witnesses.

Saturday, 12th Feb.—I was invited this day by my Greek master, Kyriacos Phaidro, to witness the celebration of vespers in the Greek church. Kyriacos is a man of very superior intellect and information, possessing a thorough knowledge of his own, and of several foreign languages. He is, indeed, a complete contrast to many of his ignorant and self-sufficient countrymen in Smyrna; although born and bred there, and, I believe, never was a dozen miles from it in his life. With that genuine love of his country, which is inseparable from a really enlightened mind, he sees and acknowledges the defects—the charlatanerie of its ecclesiastical constitutions; and laments the want of unanimity evident in its political career. Besides giving instruction in Greek, he acts as clerk to a Levant merchant here; and thus contrives to eke out a very narrow income by the most unremitting and well-directed industry.

Unfortunately we did not arrive till the ceremony was half finished. The archbishop was in his chair of state, and in the act of consecrating a quantity of bread, surrounded by a croud of "worshippers." Six immense cakes were brought forward in a basket, in which was a seventh of moderate size, which was blessed and set apart for the primate's own supper; the rest were *supposed* to be distributed among the poor. But I am well informed, that the priests themselves, unwilling that so gross an aliment should feed their flock, bestow on them benedictions *en masse,* but retain the cakes for their own private use. These facts prove how much every modification of the Catholic religion is capable of being perverted; and how little the honesty of a body of men so regulated and so maintained is to be depended on: but this is a question I have no design to pursue. I know it may give occasion to a hundred remarks; but I know also that it may be well and sufficiently upheld; here I shall leave it.

The Greek episcopal croisier is unlike that of Rome. Each side is formed by the twisted head of a serpent, in a manner like the following:

On departing, the archbishop took up a small cross, a few inches in length, and waved it, while he bestowed his blessing on the assembled people. I caught his eye several times; and, as it afterwards appeared, was the cause of some questions and curiosity. He enquired of Kyriacos why he had not introduced me to him; and bade him remember, that his house was open to every Englishman, and to every friend of *his*. I was glad to find my Greek master stand so well with his "DESPOT." The archbishop is an old man, of rather a venerable appearance; and shews more of the *gentleman* than the majority of his cloth in this country.

From hence we went to the church of the Armenians; but again we were too late. They were just dispersing. I observed, however, a custom which prevails here every Saturday, called, in Greek, μνημόσυνος, or the day of memorial. The church-yard was absolutely covered with small chafing-dishes, into which was thrown a compound of rosin and myrrh, intended, as an Armenian priest, whom we questioned, said, " for the gain of the living, and remembrance of the dead." They suppose that the souls of the departed take pleasure in seeing the cloud rise upward from the grave, bearing with it the prayers and reminiscences of the friends whom they have

loved; and in truth the observance is as harmless as any that I have noticed. It may serve
to recal the heart from its wanderings, and
convince it of its frailness and mortality. At
least, if the frequency of the occurrence does
not weaken the effect, it may soothe and soften
the mind when it renews its intercourse with
the world, by presenting images of the most
grateful order, by flattering it with holding a
sort of direct communication with the spirits
" of just men made perfect," and by filling it
with the hope of walking securely in the same
path, and of preserving in turn the same connexions it has loved and left. They have
ample faith for all this. When I asked the
priest upon what ground they performed the
ceremony, he said, " It was a tradition which
they had received from their fathers, and it
was his duty to perform it without seeking for
a reason." The composition which they burn,
is put up into small paper parcels, and provided by the priests, who charge a few paras
for each portion. A sort of money-till stands
beside the basket. On a stone, forming part
of a fountain, opposite the gate of the Armenian church, is an ancient Greek inscription,

which I had not time to copy.   This I regret
the less, as in all probability it will be given
hereafter by Mr. Arundell.

Sunday, 13th Feb.—We hear that the vice-
consul of this place, (a merchant,) and his
family, are to have a passage with us to Malta!
People have positively no consciences, though
certain of them have abundant officiousness,
self-conceit, and ridiculous pretensions.

> " Like to the bending shoulders of our anticks,
>   Who seem as they'd supported the foundation
>   Of an imperious structure, when, God wot!
>   Those arched cielings, rafters, beams, and all
>   Would feel th' weight of their grandeur and decline
>   To moulder'd earth that had no *firmer* ground-works
>   To buttress their rare fabric : So did th' Fly
>   I' th' fable glory, that she raised the dust
>   Those spoke-wheels fanned.   Thus tho' sense forbid it,
>   A self-opinion ever thinks she did it."

The Franks in Smyrna are, to this day, the
very same that they were in the days of Anas-
tasius; and what they then were, the reader
may perceive by the subjoined extract.

" In that trucking, trafficking city, peoples'
ideas run upon nothing but merchandize: their
discourse only varies between the exchanges

and the markets: their heads are full of figs and raisins, and their whole hearts wrapped up in cotton and broad-cloths. They suppose man created for nothing but to buy and sell; and whoever makes not these occupations the sole business of his life, seems to them to neglect the end of his existence. I verily believe, that they marry for no other purpose but to keep up the race of merchants."

Would that we were at Malta!

Monday, 14th Feb.—I have as yet said nothing of Greek literature; but it will hereafter form a prominent part of my observations. Notwithstanding the depressed state of the times, and the lamentable ignorance of those who are appointed to instruct the vulgar, there are not wanting distinguished examples of learning among the ecclesiastical body, by far the least inquiring portion of the community. But superstition and prejudice chain them in almost indissoluble bonds; and never, it is to be feared, will knowledge flourish, until a more enlightened character of religion becomes prevalent,—until she is freed from the galling shackles with which bigotry and slavery have encompassed her. Decidedly, however, the spirit of improvement is struggling against her oppressors, and will, no doubt, conquer at last. I have obtained, in Smyrna, by great good luck, several Hellenic performances of uncommon interest; and I shall now proceed to lay before the reader some account of them, and as far as I can, of their authors. But the fear of incurring the heaviest penalties, has obliged the most part to publish these works anonymously: information, therefore, can only be collected accidentally, and in detached and minute portions.

The first which I shall notice, is the translation of Moliere's " *Avare*," published at Vienna in 1816, by a Greek Presbyter of Smyrna, called Οἰκονόμος, or *Economus*. There is a good deal of interest attached to this person's history. He was originally a schoolmaster at Smyrna, and greatly esteemed for his many rare and uncommon endowments. The establishment prospered under his hands; and it is owing chiefly to him, that the present reviving taste for literary pursuits has made such progress among the Greeks. He was also an eloquent and able preacher; several of his sermons have been translated into various foreign lan-

11

guages, especially a funeral sermon upon the last patriarch of the Greeks ; who having subjected himself to the suspicions of the Sultan, was strangled, and clad in his pontifical habit, tied up in a sack, and thrown into the sea. A merchant vessel, on its way to Smyrna, discovered the body, and conveyed it thither, where it was sumptuously interred.

The fame and attention which Economus attracted, excited the envy of one or two Smyrniote bishops ; and his unprejudiced way of thinking drew upon him the censure of the ignorant, and the calumny of the malicious. " Οἱ συμπολῖται μου Σμυρναῖοι," he has made Zoetza say, in his comedy above mentioned, " φυσικὰ ἀγαποῦν νὰ καταλαλοῦν." It is the same at this day : the Franks complain of it, and accuse them of propagating the most unfounded tales. But whether the Franks do not equally deserve the charge, and whether it be not the common misfortune of all places where the population have little beside their neighbours' affairs to concern them, I shall not pretend to determine. Certain it is, that Economus felt the full force of their industrious mischief. With the usual persuasion of superstitious and uneducated times, they construed his experiments in chemistry into magic; and he was actually forbidden by the Turkish government to instruct his pupils in mathematics, under the apprehension (how they stumbled upon it is a mystery) that it was a vehicle for training them in the art of war. This was about three years ago, nearly a twelvemonth after the breaking out of the Greek Revolution. But imputations of this nature he might probably have overcome, had he not, unhappily, during Lent, when greatly reduced by sickness, had recourse to diet more strengthening and nutritious than accords with the regulations of a Greek fast. This proved his overthrow. Aware of the prejudice so rife with those of his persuasion, under whatever circumstance, he used the forbidden food as privately as possible; but his servant discovered the abomination, and revealed it immediately to his superiors. The envious bestirred themselves in fanning the spark; and clamoured in the most outrageous fashion. The consequence was, that he retired to Constantinople, and submitted his case to the Patriarch. *He* judged of it so lightly, that knowing

the high talents and scientific character of the
exiled priest, he sent him back, with letters to
the archbishop, commanding that he should
be reinstated in his former offices. The people
were accordingly convoked, and the Metropolitan church fixed on as the place of meeting. The primate ascended his chair, and
read to them the orders of the Patriarch ; but
so inflamed were the minds of the populace,
so surprizingly had they been worked upon by
the arts of priestcraft, that they rushed forward, snatched up the written mandate, and
tore it into a thousand pieces ! So violent an
ebullition of popular fervour, in a country so
superstitious, and enslaved as this, never perhaps was recorded in the pages of history !
Economus yielded to its fury, and returned
again to Constantinople, where he entered into
the service of a Greek Dragoman to the Porte,
whom he assisted in the discharge of his official
duties.

But the disasters of the persecuted priest
terminated not here. The Dragoman incurred
the displeasure of the Sultan, and he, with his
whole household, were put under an arrest. It
seems, that in cases of this kind, the Patriarch

is made responsible for the persons of the offenders. He is to guard them at his own cost, and to answer for their escape, to the higher powers. Accordingly, the Dragoman and his family were confined to their own house under the custody of a caloyer, one of the lowest order of Greek monks, whom they easily contrived to elude. They pledged his reverence so heartily, in some right orthodox beverage, that he was soon no longer in a condition to oppose their flight. By the aid of Economus, they had engaged a Russian vessel to carry them away; but it happened, that though they all got safely on board, contrary winds precluded every possibility of sailing. In due time the monk recovered from his fit of intoxication; and having ascertained that the prisoners had uncourteously left him alone, he sallied hastily forth to disclose his negligence and inebriety to his principal. The Patriarch carried the story to the Vizier, and the Vizier to the Sultan, " then curled his very beard for ire," and orders were sent off to the admiral of the port to make diligent search for the fugitives. The emissaries went three times on board the very vessel in which they were concealed; but through the influence, or more properly, the money of Count Strogonoff, the Russian minister, (who is said, much to his honour, to have contributed largely to their escape, and whom they had, by some means or other, apprized of their situation), they got off undiscovered to St. Petersburgh, where Economus now resides.

Moliere's play of " L'Avare," is adapted to Hellenic manners and ideas. The scene is placed in Smyrna, and the characters each speak in dialects proper to them. They are thus described :

1. Exentavelones, the father of Cleanthes and Zoetza.

2. Varthalambumba, father of Chariclea and Demetrius.

3. Cleanthes, son of Exentavelones, and lover of Chariclea.

4. Zoetza, daughter of Exentavelones.

5. Demetrius, the adopted son of Varthalambumba, and lover of Zoetza. [His name is properly *Demetraces*, a diminutive of Demetrius ; as from *man, manekin* ; a little man, Zoetza is similarly formed.]

6. Chariclea, daughter of Varthalambumba.

7. Keratza Sophoulio, a female go-between, [Προξενήτρια, literally, *a marriage-broker*.]

8. Mr. Simos, a messenger.

9. Mr. Giannes, (or John,) cook to Exenta-velones.

10. Mrs. Maria, maid-servant to Exentave-lones.

11. Vrakes, gardener to Exentavelones.

12. Mrs. Kakoula, a poor tenant of Exenta-velones.

13. Stroveles, servant to Cleanthes.

14. Wardens ['Επίτροποι] of the hospital.

15. Archelaus, principal public secretary.

Of these characters, the third, fourth, fifth, and sixth, speak in the best dialect of Smyrna, which is superior even to that spoken in the Fanal of Constantinople, and so much extolled. In the latter place, a vast number of Turkish words are mingled with the Greek; but in Smyrna it is more pure.

The first, second, seventh, tenth, eleventh, and twelfth, are also of the dialect of Smyrna, but appropriated exclusively to the lower order of uneducated persons. The ninth is a dialect of Macedonia, or rather of Thessaly, as the

author hints in his Preface : and the thirteenth
of the Island of Scio.   Economus also wrote
an original tragedy, which has been acted ;
and a comedy which is still in manuscript.

I have met with an original play, a rhyming
tragedy, called "POLYXENA, *composed by the
most noble gentleman, Mr. Jacob Rizos, otherwise called Neroulos."* This is certainly a step
in Grecian literature.   The tragedy was *acted*
three times in Smyrna, and oftener in Constantinople.   They had a part of the Spanish
consul's house prepared for the purpose,
with costumes adapted to the parts that were
represented.   But all this was disturbed by
the Revolution ; and a copy of the drama
is of the last degree of scarcity.   It was procured with the utmost difficulty by the worthy
Kyriacos.

Lord Byron, in the Appendix to his first
part of Childe Harold, mentions, that " Chris-
todoulos, an Acarnanian, has published, in
Vienna, some physical treatises in Hellenic."
I have obtained a work, by the same author,
published at Vienna in 1811, entitled " Laoni-
cus and Zantippe ; or, the Faithful Lover and

Imprudent Mother. A drama, in two parts." It is written in prose, and forms a sort of dramatic history, each division containing four long acts.

The "Temistocle" of Metastasio, printed at Vienna, in 1796, by George Ventole, " now first printed," says the title-page, " at the expence and by the care of Polyzoes Lampanitziotes, of Ioannina; is translated by an anonymous writer, (Παρὰ του Κυρίου . . . .) in prose. The translation is by no means literal.

The "*Olympiade*," by the same Italian poet, is also anonymously translated into Greek heroic couplets, " E'N 'ΟΦΕΝΗ," 1815; intermingled with songs. It is ornamented with very indifferent vignettes, cut in wood. Marmontel's "*Shepherdess of the Alps*," versified chiefly in the irregular measure of the Italian sonnet; and " *The First Mariner, a Poem, in two Cantos, by the German Poet Gesner, translated into our Tongue by Antonius, tle Son of Koronius*," are in the same volume, of 204 duodecimo pages. The latter is in prose.

The last work which I obtained at this time is an *original* Hellenic composition, with the following title, " Certain Dramatic Poems, composed by George, the Son of Nicholas Soutzos, formerly Grand [μεγάλος] Interpreter of the powerful Ottoman Empire. At the expence of that most useful gentleman Eustathius Mitze. In the year 1805. By the care of Theodosius of Ioannina." What is singular, it bears at the bottom of the page the notification in Italian " CON REGIA APPROVAZIONE." But whose may be the royal approbation is a matter of no small doubt.

This collection is curious. There are four pieces, of which the first is called " ΤΟ ΑΣΥΛΟΝ ΤΟΥ ΦΘΟΝΟΥ," *The Asylum of Envy*, in three short acts, partly composed in verse, and partly in prose. The names of the actors are—

> WISDOM,
> RICHES,
> CONSANGUINITY,
> VIRTUE,
> SIN, the mother of Envy,
> ENVY, the son of Sin,
>   and the
> CHORUS.

The next bears the title of the " Illuminated Courtier," and represents the following characters :

THE COURTIER,

LOVE OF TRUTH,

DECEIT, under the appearance and in the name of VIRTUE.

AMBITION, under the appearance and in the name of HONOUR.

VENALITY, under the appearance and in the name of FRIENDSHIP.

It is comprised in two acts, and is entirely prose.

The third part of the volume is called " The Country of Fools," in three acts. The description of the *dramatis personæ* is singular;

MANIARCHES, the leader of the fools,

POTAMORRYTOS, the prodigal fool,

VRONTOKROTOS, the irritable fool,

CHREMATOPHILOS, the covetous fool,

KALLIANCHIA, the vain female fool,

TERPSITHYMOS, the gay (or noisy) female fool,

and

Servants, who do not speak.

This piece is composed chiefly in prose, but there are rhyming passages scattered about.

The fourth division is perhaps the most curious of the whole : it is denominated " *The*

Catechumen; or the Cosmogonical Theatre,"
and relates to the various opinions of ancient
philosophers respecting the origin of the world.
Adam and *Moses* are among the number.

Dramatis Personæ.

CATECHUMEN, or *Student,*

ANAXAGORAS,

ARISTOTLE,

EPICURUS,

A DISCIPLE OF EPICURUS,

CARTESIUS, [Des Cartes,]

NEWTON, [NEYΘΩN, pronounced *Nevthon,*]

ADAM,

MOSES.

In the second act, at the conclusion of the
fourth scene, the Catechumen, after listening
to the arguments of Newton, remarks, "Τουτο
το σύστημά σου μοὶ ἐφάνη καὶ πιθανώτερον, καὶ
προκριτώτερον των λοιπων· ὅθεν καὶ υποσχομαι
επὶ ζωῆς μου νὰ τὸ ἔχω εγκεχαραγμὲνον εἰς
τὴν καρδίαν μου. Φευγει *." Finally, however, he declares for the system of Moses,

---

* " This system of yours appears to me both more
probable and more eligible than the rest: therefore, I
promise, through my life, to hold it deeply engraved
within my heart.—*He goes out.*"

which he pronounces " τὸ τελειότερον, καὶ τὸ θειότερον ὅλων τῶν λοιπῶν παλαιῶν τε καὶ νεωτέρων *."

It is written in prose, and contains three acts.

* " The most perfect, and the most divine of all others, old and new."

CHAPTER VIII.

TUESDAY, 15*th Feb.*—Preparations made for leaving Smyrna, the quarantine flag already hoisted. Besides the family of the vice-consul aforesaid, and three or four families of Greeks, we have another passenger, a Mr. Bulwer, one of the agents for the Greek committee, apparently in the last stage of consumption. Mr. Bulwer came out from England several months ago in company with Mr. Hamilton Browne. They landed at Napoli, where the first of these gentlemen caught the yellow fever. We hear that the Greeks took advantage of his unhappy situation to pilfer him on all sides; his Greek physician demanded and received *two hundred dollars* for his assistance, and the government required him to decamp immediately, lest he should spread the contagion farther. And this was done to persons who entered the country expressly for the purpose of negotiating a loan, and of rendering such other assistance as their situation called for ! All I can say of the story at present is, that it wants proof. As yet I have had no opportunity of communicating with him. Mr. Bulwer went from Napoli to Smyrna, where he has been most humanely and kindly entertained by the English consul for four or five months. It is said he is *sick of the Greeks !* Alas ! Alas !

Wednesday, 16*th Feb.*——Sailed this morning from Smyrna and anchored at Vourla, where we shall stay some days. The Cyrene is to take in water. Our destination is Malta, which will require twenty-five days quarantine.

Monday, 21*st Feb.*——Still off Vourla, waiting for the return of the Seringapatam. We are in strict quarantine, and not even permitted, as we anticipated, the pleasure of shooting on an uninhabited island close by. Last Saturday we were amused by witnessing some of the lower deck guns fired at a mark.

Our station is extremely beautiful : we lie in a sort of gulf, surrounded on three quarters by six small islands like dots upon a circle. Upon the fourth rise the lofty mountains of

Asia, and the well cultivated country beneath. Peering over the islands are other remote mountains silvered with snow, and illumined by a bright sun.

The Greek prisoners have been judiciously set to the pumps, and otherwise employed in the ship. They seem cheerful and unconcerned at their situation, being in all likelihood better lodged and fed than they have ever before been accustomed to. I regret that I sometimes overhear expressions of bitterness and animosity against them fall from the sailors; they appear to consider these unfortunate men as beings of another class, and scarcely entitled to the common obligations of humanity. Whilst the blood shed in the conflict was yet undried, one might not perhaps blame some sudden ebullitions of this kind; or we might find in the mournful spectacle, presented by the death of their comrades, a partial justification. But one is sorry to hear an Englishman, of whatever station, indulge a protracted and cowardly spleen; and still more sorry must we be to perceive it, as I have perceived it, extend even to the inanimate body of the dead! A few days ago, one of the

Greeks who had been wounded by a sabre stroke across the head, expired, and the sailor engaged in preparing the corpse for its last home, treated it in a manner so vindictive and revolting as to call down a severe reproof from the officer who was superintending the arrangement! It was worthy of a more touching castigation!

Uneducated and boisterous men, it is true, are not expected to discover much delicacy or much feeling, but common decency it is right to demand from them. The pirates were well worthy of their fate, but once subjected to it all further exhibition of hostility should cease—we are not called upon to pursue even the wicked to extremity, but this is frequently overlooked or not attended to by the educated and refined. It has happened to me, more than once, to hear many well-meaning people express themselves, respecting wicked men, in terms of inveteracy, which no Christian can or ought to approve. A late illustrious and (spite of his many failings, I will add) lamented poet, has remarked that " None are *all* evil," and it does not demand a very profound knowledge of the human mind to arrive at the same

truth. The fact is, they cannot be so—the un-
restrained violence of some particular passion
will oftentimes impel them unconsciously towards virtue. The wild daring of the robber
gives a kind of savage generosity to his character which an honester man may not possess : he will carelessly fling his gold to the
wretch whom poverty has stripped, though it
may have been attained by bloodshed and the
imminent jeopardy of his own dark existence.
The man who would rejoice to steal away your
reputation will shrink from actual robbery.
He who would wind himself around the unsus-
pecting heart, and sting it unto death, will not
become indeed a murderer : there is a barrier
of pride, perhaps of fear, which rises up against
it ;—there is the bias of prejudice—there is the
current of opinion, and the bulwarks of situation and circumstance,—there is, in reality, all
that contributes to form one vice, opposed, and
vigorously opposed, to another. As we cannot
be wholly good, neither can we be wholly vi-
cious. The Roman Emperor, placed on the
summit of cruelty as well as power, who wished
that the human race had but one head that it
might be sundered at a blow, expressed but his

incapacity to be as evil as his will. And could he have achieved it, the operation of that horrid crime would have effectually precluded the commission of another; it would have left him amidst an unpeopled world, a solitary monster, the despot of a wilderness, and the lord of one wide cemetery. Yet even towards him, as the historian * relates, the most delicate mark of feeling which affection could devise was exhibited. Flowers were scattered upon his tomb at the very moment when public odium was busiest with his memory, and his barbarities were yet fresh upon their minds. There had then been some good deed which called forth the honest tribute ; and the oppressed and labouring waters which had so long flowed on in darkness felt a gleam of momentary sunshine ! The first Richard of England commanded and witnessed in cool blood the execution of three thousand Turks ; yet the archer whose shaft put a period to his martial frenzy, he had generosity enough not only to pardon but reward !——These are not isolated facts ; they are supported by innumerable evidences, both of

* Suetonius.

ancient history and the experience of every day, although it be most true that while

> " The evil that men do lives after them,
> The *good* is oft interred with their bones."

They call upon us, therefore, to regard the wicked, not as being too bad to be redeemed, but as being bad enough to need our warning voice, our helping hand; to believe them not such as we may virtuously persecute for their wickedness, but such as we may confidently hope our exertions may awaken, and our earnestness retrieve. To take the worst light, whether of men or actions, is not, to say the least, the most charitable part; and it is but a small degree removed from the vanity of self-applause, and the pride of conscious superiority!

I have been led unwillingly into this subject, but it can hardly be thought an unnecessary digression. And if I have suggested any thing which may check the impulses of an outrageous animosity, or obviate the poisonous virulence with which some delight to bespatter frail humanity, I shall not lament the occasion which has led to it.

Monday Noon. — The Seringapatam just arrived : she has been at Hydra and Spetzia, as well as at Milo. The Greek government at Hydra, we hear, has provided two fine Arabian horses for Captain Hamilton, as a testimony of the great esteem in which he is held. It is thus that his enlightened and humane policy secures the respect and approbation of all parties;—Turks, Greeks, and Franks!

Thursday, 24th Feb.—Sailed from Vourla with a light wind. Two of our passengers were turned over to the Seringapatam, the Hon. Mr. Strangways, and MR. HALL. The latter gentleman left England with us intending to go no further than Gibraltar; but our company proved so agreeable to him, that he has remained ever since. Happy Cambrian! when she can produce so unquestionable a testimonial of good conduct! May the Seringapatam prove as happy!!

With Mr. Strangways I feel loth to part, as I always do with a well-informed and gentlemanly man; and it seems probable, that we shall meet again at Smyrna. Our eternal *old friend*, MR. HALL, likewise anticipates this particular pleasure; and I doubt not, although

s 2

it is " *absolutely requisite* that he should return home in June," that he will be delighted
to renew his intimacy with us (US of the Cambrian!) at the same place, in that, or in any
one given month of the year! " But its Jove's
doing ; and Jove make us thankful !" We have
been much incommoded by the number of the
passengers ; and the difficulty of finding them
births is not small. I cannot, in this place, forbear throwing out a hint to those who may
hereafter be favoured with a passage in a man-
of-war, not to consider themselves as sailing in
a public conveyance ; nor to assume such a de-
portment as may authorise a conclusion, that
they think themselves conferring a favour,
rather than receiving one. I would also hum-
bly suggest, that to press upon the good-nature
of the Captain, even when it is obviously contrary to his inclination——to solicit a passage
for one port, and being arrived, to require it
for " another, and another, and another," is as
indelicate as for any one to come a mere
stranger to your house, and, finding the quarters good, there to set up his rest. The cases
are perfectly similar ; and it seems to me to
imply such a total want of proper feeling, as

to render those, who are thus deficient, objects
of merited contempt.   I cannot, for my part,
comprehend the principle on which they act.
A person is slightly introduced to a Captain
of a man-of-war, in order to obtain a gra-
tuitous present of bed and board.   The cost
is wholly on the side of the commander;
and if he be not a man of independent fortune, he has to endure a tax upon his income, which he can perhaps very hardly support.   Besides this, he is obliged to surrender
his own comforts to the encroachments of his
passengers, who, in many cases, think themselves entitled to the attention which they
would exact from the hired servant of a
packet-boat.

What I have here said, I wish to be understood as a common feeling among the
officers of a man-of-war; and without meaning
to impute any thing further to particular indi-
viduals than inexperience and want of consideration, it may be useful to future voyagers,
to understand in what light their presence is
considered, and how they are expected to act.
We have, indeed, several distinguished exceptions to the method upon which I have ani-

madverted; but I am persuaded some comment is needed for the rest: and I hope it will be taken in good part.

With regard to the ward-room passengers, a system somewhat different is, for various reasons, adopted: but here too, I have seen more than one individual conduct himself as he would, where not only a full equivalent was paid, but where his superiority of rank authorized an unceremonious disposal of whatsoever he might desire. Such practices never will be tolerated in a man-of-war; at least, not on a peace establishment, when the officers are generally men of fortune and family. For the present I quit the subject; if I should see occasion, it shall certainly be resumed.

The Seringapatam is to cruise up and down the islands, and to take the part that would have been taken by the Cambrian had she not received the damage before alluded to. It is extremely annoying to have seen just enough of these places to augment my avidity for research and travel, and then to be carried off and detained elsewhere, one knows not how long! Our next voyage will, I hope, be more fortunate.

Friday, 25th Feb.——About noon Negropont appeared upon our starboard bow. The name of this island has been most singularly corrupted. Originally *Eubæa,* it has, by the change of the Greek pronounciation of the letters Eu and b, into *Ef* and *v,* been converted into *Efvæa, Efripo* or *Evripo, Egripo, Negripo, Negripont ;* which last has, I imagine, (with Wheeler and Hobhouse) been derived by confounding the three Greek words, εἰς τὸν Ἔγριπον, abbreviated in the vulgar dialect to ᾿στὸν Ἔγριπον, and pronounced as one word.

A little after three o'clock we anchored in Port Mandri, near which Dr. Sibthorp noticed the ruins of a temple and the remains of an ancient town *. But his accounts are always meagre and unsatisfactory. Unfortunately our quarantine prevents any communication with the shore at present. A Maltese brig, at anchorage in this place, informs us, that she fell in with the Turkish fleet, consisting of twenty-seven sail, off Patras, a few days ago.

Saturday, 26th Feb.——Passed Cape Colonna

* See *Walpole's Travels in Greece.* Vol. II. p. 34.

at an early hour this morning. The day broke rainy and cheerless; and the white pillars of the temple necessarily lost somewhat of their beauty from the dense atmosphere through which they were seen. But I distinguished enough to remember the " *Bellona Austriaca*," and to anathematize her with due energy. This vessel is stationed at Smyrna; and it was our lot to see something of her officers at the Casino there. I would keep within bounds, and leave a portion of their merits to be guessed at by the sagacious reader: I will only say, therefore, that a greater set of bears never danced at a fair, or scribbled upon a column! And it is comfortable to reflect, that such really *was* the description of persons who had wantonly defaced a noble monument!

Anchored toward evening in *Garden Bay*, about six miles from Hydra: it rained violently, with some lightning. Last voyage a boat belonging to the Cambrian upset, in its way back from Hydra, in consequence of a sudden squall: all the crew, with the exception of three sailors, were lost.

Sunday, 27th Feb.——The celebrated Greek Admiral Miaoulis, accompanied by his secretary, came along-side the Cambrian, about two o'clock, for the purpose of conversing with Captain Hamilton. He is a grey-headed man, of about sixty years ; of large but rather coarse features. His face, however, is far from bad; and his frame is bulky, and knit with the appearance of uncommon strength. A blue capote, lined with scarlet, covered a dress of brown cloth, fashioned after the national taste. He wore the common light scull-cap of his country, and grey mustachios decorated the upper lip. His appearance in a boat resembling a fisherman's, attended only by two or three sailors, together with the homely exterior which he presented, gave one no very lofty conception of the admiral of a Greek fleet ! But there might be policy in this : he might wish as few auditors of what passed between him and the captain, as possible ; and might think, with Petruchio, that

> " 'Tis the mind that makes the body rich ;
>   And as the sun breaks thro' the darkest clouds,
>   So honour peereth in the meanest habit."

To say truth, it is one of the greatest weaknesses of humanity to be caught by the tinsel of adventitious circumstances. Such hold,

however, has it upon the vulgar of all denomi-
nations; and so imperceptibly does it insinuate
itself into the minds even of those who look
farther than the superficies, that there are few
upon whom the impression is not made; and
its effect is often in full activity, when the
cause has ceased to be remembered, or acknowledged.   It is the " feathers green and
gold," that occasion many an unprofitable two-
legged thing to pass muster, and to assume a
rank very far beyond its merit.   It is this that
enshrines it in public opinion.   It is this that
lightens up the most gloomy portions of human character, and throws an artificial sunshine over the vilest relations of life !   But
who knows it not ?   Can we pass from one
threshold to another without observing it ?
Can the eye, possessing all its faculties, avoid
distinguishing what has dyes so vivid, and
magnitude so immense ?   Here men may need
a monitor, but not information ; they may
think little of what long use has rendered
familiar; but they cannot be ignorant of its
presence, or of its power !——Enough.

The admiral, Miaoulis, expressed himself disappointed at Captain Hamilton's intention to

decline the horses which they were preparing to present to him. This, for private reasons, it was judged better to do; and Miaoulis therefore testified some reluctance in accepting a beautifully engraved medal of George IV. which the captain had received from our ambassador at Naples, and which bore some reference, on the obverse side, to the present state of Greece. It was of little value, although of admirable execution. Ultimately it was received. The Greek intimated that as soon as the government at Hydra learnt from the Seringapatam the defeat and capture of the pirates by our ships, they immediately sent out a schooner of war to cruise in that quarter : whether for the purpose of ascertaining on the spot what had passed, or perhaps of putting a stop to future piracies. The number of their squadron destined to oppose the Turks, he stated at forty vessels. But they had not as yet recommenced operations, although aware that the Turkish fleet had quitted the harbour and were sailing in pursuit of them. In opposition to this authentic communication, it may be amusing to subjoin an extract or two from Galignani's Messenger, dated 21st. Dec. 1824.

" Extract of a private letter of the 8th inst. from Trieste :—' An Austrian vessel from the Mediterranean has arrived at this port. On the 8th Nov. it met off Candia the Greek fleet, which had just gained another victory over Ibrahim Pacha, commander of the naval forces of the Turks. The following is an extract of a letter relative to the affair, written by an officer of the Greek navy to one of his friends at Trieste :—

" On board the admiral's ship off Crete,
" *Nov,* 8,

" ' The checks which Ibrahim Pacha experienced off Cos, in the channel of Scio, and off Mitylene were the more deeply felt by him, as, in a fit of Mussulman bravado, he had promised *by his beard* to reduce the Isle of Hydra in seven hours, and immediately to turn his victorious arms upon the Morea, which he expected to subject to his authority in a month. Upon returning into the Gulf of Halicarnassus (Boudroun) he redoubled his efforts to effect a disembarkation in the Isle of Crete, in order to repair, in some degree, his humiliating losses. Scarcely had he set sail for that destination when *our admiral,* who watched all his movements, went in pursuit of him. We came up with the enemy between Crete and Casos. *Twenty of his vessels* were captured, and others sunk. Nearly *two thousand men of the Egyptian troops called regulars* fell into our hands, and many others were drowned. The rest of the Mussulman fleet is dispersed.

(Signed) " MALEAS.' "

Galignani's Messenger, December 24.

" The defeat of Ibrahim Pacha by the Greek squadron off Crete is confirmed by *letters from Constantinople* and other places."

These forgeries are the more ridiculous when we remember the size of the Greek vessels, and consequently, the almost moral impossibility of such a capture as is here spoken of. Not a ship of the Greek squadron now in Hydra probably exceeds 150 tons. The lofty Pouqueville too, who always writes as though his head touched heaven——and indeed it often *is* among the clouds——speaking of Hydra observes " Cette île possédait en 1816 quarante vaisseaux du port de *quatre cents à six cents tonneaux* construits dans ses chantiers, avec des pins d'Olympie." Admitting the bare possibility of such a circumstance *then*, it is out of all reach of possibility *now*; and though they could be built, it is most certain that at present they could not be equipped.

A conversation which I have had to-day with Mr. Bulwer, satisfies me as to the inaccuracy of the information before hinted at relative to the government of Napoli. They shewed them all the civility in their power, though from the disastrous circumstances of the period, they were incapable of doing much. What he chiefly complains of, is their tardiness in giving definitive answers to the proposals, and the petty intrigues which they seemed to be carrying on. Perhaps he may be right; but surely he was wrong when he embarked for a remote country like Greece in the very worst state of a revolutionary epoch, expecting (as it appears to me he did) to find accommodations in travelling similar to those of his own country! His servants are raw inexperienced Frenchmen, to whom he leaves all the arrangements of his journey; and they being equally ignorant and careless, are provided scarcely with one single requisite. They carry coffee with them, but no means of grinding it; a few eggs, but, I believe, no utensil for cooking them. Now every man who knows any thing of Greece, knows well that apparatus of all kinds must be conveyed along with the traveller, and that he must depend entirely upon his own resources for his "daily bread." Unhappily, Mr. Bulwer has dearly bought his experience; but it is unfair to stigmatize the Greeks for the improvidence of himself or his attendants.

The Greeks, to whom Captain Hamilton's kindness permitted a passage in the ship, were put on board the boat of their admiral to be conveyed to Hydra. Our prisoners had imagined that they also would be landed in the same place, but finding their mistake several of them burst into tears. One man in particular exhibited very considerable agitation, and thrusting his head out of a port-hole, bawled lustily to his countrymen for aid. His entreaties and tears were equally ineffectual.

Monday, *28th Feb.*——The REBEL Celoco-troni, as I omitted to observe before, is de-

10

tained a prisoner in a convent a little above the town of Hydra.

Tuesday, 1st March—The Seringapatam has made us a signal this evening to say that the Greeks have gained a splendid victory over the Turkish fleet off Navarin, a place of considerable importance, not far from the Gulf of Coron. This communication is said to have been made by a boat from Hydra. The circumstance, if true, is extremely gratifying, but it wants confirmation.

Wednesday, 2d March—Sailed early from Garden Bay with a fair wind toward Malta. Passed Spetzia about noon.

Thursday, 3d March — In sight of the Island of Sapienza, about thirty miles from the place described as the scene of the naval victory just gained by the Greeks. Several English and Austrian merchant ships cruising about.

Friday, 4th March—A beautiful morning; the state of the atmosphere is considerably changed; "the time of the singing of birds is come, and the voice of the turtle is heard in our land." The mountains of Arcadia in sight.

Tuesday Evening, 8th March.—Arrived at Malta, that " military hot-house," as it has been not inaptly called. The appearance which it presents from the sea is always new and inviting. We had to-day rather a different aspect; and I thought La Valetta resembled a town chiselled out of the rock, to which the skilful hand of the lapicide had but just given the finishing touch. Malta is famous for vases cut from the same soft porous stone; and I could easily have fancied that the clean yellow cast of the houses and churches, rising over this the most precipitous part of the island, was devised by a sculptor, and executed *con amore !* Let not my faith be quarrelled with, I have no wish to impose it upon others; he who proposed cutting Mount Athos into a monument for the son of Philip, had, perhaps, an imagination equally lively.

We have yet ten days to remain in quarantine, (*thirty* being the allotted number instead of twenty-five as we supposed,) unless the situation of the Cambrian induce the Board of Health to shorten our durance.

Thursday, 10th March.—To-day Captain Hamilton read a letter from the admiral, approving of the capture of the pirates, and stating his intention to represent the conduct of all concerned in a favourable light to the Admiralty. The Dock people are removing such of the Cambrian's stores as are not liable to communicate infection. This is preparatory to her being *hove down*.

Tuesday, 15th March.—We were released from quarantine—a most joyful circumstance. To be cooped up in our " winged citadel" at sea is nothing ; we expect no other, and our minds are made up to the endurance ; but to be so imprisoned in harbour, with the prospect of an augmented society before us—with the power of roaming at pleasure from place to place—" from flower to flower," just as inclination prompts ; all in sight, yet all withheld, is realizing the fable of Tantalus, and tempting us to wish the right honourable Board of Health a hearty ducking !

As soon as I could make it convenient to land I set out in pursuit of lodgings ; there is indeed a place appropriated to the officers of a man of war during repairs of this nature. It is called the *Lofts*, and it might as well have been called the *Lights*, for it is very *low* and

13

very *dark;* but *" lucus à* NON *lucendo"* is not in these days so remarkable a cognomen! " Things change their titles as our manners turn ;" and of a surety, never age, in comparison with another, has proved itself so mutable as this.

Friday, 18*th March.*—The account of our expedition against the pirates I find in the *Malta Gazette,* a weekly (also a *weakly*) paper, reserved entirely for the promulgation of the edicts of government. It is said likewise that Ibrahim Pacha has landed 6,000 men at Modon, near Navarin. The information was brought by a Maltese vessel.

Sunday, 20*th March.*——Preached at the Chapel of the Palace, on the subject of *Conversation.* Malta, like all other places where time hangs heavy upon peoples' hands, is noted for its propensity to scandal ; and the zeal with which the affairs of others are canvassed in preference to their own. My observations made a little stir—a slight sensation, and—— were forgotten ere night-fall !

Tuesday, 22*d March.*——To-day the Cambrian was hove down, and all the fair and the young and the high-born honoured us with a

T 2

visit. She (that is the ship) lay with her keel out of water, and exhibited her wounds to the admiring damsels. Let us hope that the Cambrian will never be insensible to the commiseration and interest shewn in her misfortunes!

Thursday, 24th March.—Rode with my friend Cleugh to Civita Vecchia, a distance of eight miles from Valetta. A high wind and dusty roads were no less a torment than the crowds of importunate *Ciceroni* who beset us on our arrival, and pursued us with the most determined coolness in spite of many urgent entreaties, and certain formidable menaces. Civita Vecchia was anciently the capital of Malta, and the chief residence of the Grand Masters. It contains some magnificent houses, now unoccupied; courts of justice which retain nothing of their original character but the usual emblems above the entrance. There is a strong fortification here, but it is also neglected; and its gates serve to enclose a warren of lazy, dirty monks, and a cathedral church of great beauty; the interior possesses a chastity of ornament quite surprising for a Catholic country. The *catacombs* are said to be worth seeing, but this I was obliged to defer until another opportunity.

Dined with Cleugh, and spent the evening at Sir Harry Neale's, where a pretty married lady (whom I strongly suspect of being a *Blue !*) told me, with a look expressing an indefinable compound of coquetry, simplicity, and pedantry, that the Sirocco wind, of which we were speaking, "*would annul salt :*"—fine words these, " prave 'ords as you shall see in a summer's day."

Ibrahim Pacha's fleet is said to be dispersed by a storm—which is likely ; for the wind has blown with extreme violence of late, insomuch that the same pretty lady above mentioned protested that it " had almost blown her out of bed !"

Saturday, 26th March.—Dined with Major General Sir Manley Power, to whose civilities I confess myself much indebted. I learnt the result of the trial, and the story of a number of Greek pirates, who, about a year ago, were captured by the Naiad. They had boarded a Maltese merchantman, murdered seventeen of her crew in cold blood, and scuttled the ship. The evidence against them was clear and decisive; but, by some extraordinary and inexplicable conceit of the jurymen, they were acquitted of the murder; and have, in consequence, been sentenced on another count to the gallies. So little did any of these wretched beings look for life, that one of them, on ascertaining that certain property found in their possession had been identified by a Maltese, hung himself in a fit of despair.

The pirates whom we secured are to be imprisoned until the case has been reported to the Admiralty: their fate will rest therefore upon the communication from England.

Major Laing, the gallant officer mentioned in the accounts of the contest with the Ashantees, was of the party mentioned above. He is about to proceed on an expedition to the Niger.

Good Friday, 1st April.—The Roman Catholics in this place have been occupied during the whole of this day, and the greater part of yesterday, in the exhibition of the most disgusting mummery that ever disgraced rational beings. Representations of our Saviour, fashioned after a manner almost too hideous to conceive, have been carried about the town, to the singular edification of all true believers. The flesh of certain of these images was of a fine *sea-green*, upon which streaks of red paint, intended to convey an idea of blood, were lavishly sprinkled. A child, cloathed in the skin of a lamb, pourtrayed, by a kind of practical blasphemy seldom paralleled, the type of our Saviour. Monks in their albs preceded them, holding lighted wax torches of immense bulk; and, in the rear of each came a number of penitents, barefooted, and clanking heavy chains attached to the ankle. These are sometimes so ponderous as to cause unspeakable pain; and the perspiration produced by the effort of dragging them along, is frequently so violent as to saturate the sack-cloth garment which completely envelopes their persons. This strange vesture reminds me of a pig in a poke; it towers at the head like a fool's cap, and has two small round holes cut in it for the especial service and gratification of the eyes. Besides the penance just noticed, there were certain folk sitting bare-breached on thorns; so at least I was told, but their naked feet were only exposed. Throughout the day nothing was to be heard but the rattling of wooden machines, which were incessantly *grinding the bones of Judas Iscariot!* A very large machine of this kind, I observed placed upon the roof of one of their churches, at which three men were laboriously employed. What could maniacs do more at variance with common sense? And what must be said for the religion which thus deprives men of their reason and consigns them to absurdity and bigotry? But above all, what can we think of its ministers, whose unremitted endeavour it is to work upon the ignorance of these poor people, and to keep alive an infatuation which leads to such deplorable results? What plea is there for them?—for those " whom methinks I see coming towards me, with a sullen gravity, as though they could not abide vice—by day-light; rudely cloathed for to witness outwardly their contempt of outward things; with books in their hands against glory, whereto they set their names; sophistically speaking against subtlety, and angry with any man in whom they see the foul fault of anger *." God be thanked, my own country at least is untainted by such abominations.

* Sir Philip Sydney's " *Defence of Poesy.*"

Instead of grinding the bones of Judas, they very properly break the bones of one another. Now this I call rational! and as to the rest of the description, I put the parallel entirely upon their own consciences—good beasts of burden are they, and will scarcely break down with the load!

Wednesday, 5th April.—Last evening was marked by a theatrical representation, in which the amateurs of the garrison were actors, in behalf of a charity. Major de Batha, Lieut. Colonel Whitmore and two of his family, enacted the principal characters; and were, indeed, intitled to them. The play was the "Midnight Hour," with the farce of "X. Y. Z." The female parts were "lively" represented by certain fair-faced youths; of whom, one copied, to admiration, the "minced speech, set look, and ginger pace," of a waiting-woman. All this is very well; and, if it go no further, is a harmless method of enlivening the dulness and varying the monotony of a garrison town. But who does not know what mischievous fire has been enkindled by the "bravos" of good-natured friends? From hence we may probably trace much of the theatrical mania of loungers

at play-houses, many connexions (of all the most
prejudicial) formed with the heroes and heroines
of the green-room : imprudent marriages, and
the best and most important period of life
trifled away, (to say no worse,) in pursuits
whose tendency is to unnerve the mind, and
leave it incapacitated for any useful or manly
occupation.   For these reasons, I confess, I
am no friend to private theatricals ; and I re-
probate, in the strongest manner, the admission of *lady*-actresses, on any grounds, into
such amusements.   In this respect, the good
sense of the *amateurs* was distinguished ; and,
I hope, always will be distinguished.   The
effect of them upon the minds and hearts of
women, is deep and lasting : and, at all events,
they introduce a vitiated taste, which seeks for
gratification among the garbage of novels and
romances.   Having turned the heart, it may
eventually turn the head, " as it sometimes
fared with a gentlewoman of our own nation,"
(I adopt the anecdote from one who, amidst
much pedantic quaintness, has read the ladies
a lecture, to which they would do well to attend ;) " who so daily bestowed the expence of
her best hours upon the stage, as being sur-

prised by sickness, even unto death, she became so deaf to such as admonished her of her end, as when her physician was to minister a receipt unto her, which he had prepared to allay the extremity of that agonizing fit wherewith she was then assailed, putting aside the receipt with her hand, as she rejected it, in the very height and heat of her distemper, with an active resolution, used these words unto her doctor,—' Thanks, good Horatio, take it for thy pains *.' "

It was amusing, after the play, to hear the encomiums bestowed upon each of the actors, as they rejoined their friends, with all their newly-acquired laurels flourishing gracefully upon them. " Your performance was excellent, admirable, inimitable,"—and so forth. Then the modest suffusion of countenance which accompanied each announcement; the pride of conscious excellence, uniting with a

* " The English Gentlewoman drawn out to the full body; expressing what habiliments do best attire her, what ornaments do best adorn her, what complements do best accomplish her." By Richard Braithwaite, Esq. London, 1641. p. 299.

beautiful reluctance to receive the homage that was rendered. My friends must pardon me for indulging in a smile, but I fancied that *this* was the better part of their acting, "admirable" as that was which preceded. So true is that which Young, if I quote correctly, has embodied in the following lines :

" The love of praise, howe'er conceal'd by art,
Glows more or less, and reigns in every heart.
The proud to gain it, toils on toils endure,
The modest shun it, but to make it sure.
It aids the dancer's skill—the writer's head,
And heaps the plain with mountains of the dead :
Nor ends it here ; it nods with sable plumes,
Shines on our hearse, and glitters on our tombs."

Thursday, 6th April.—The *conversazione* of the Marchioness of Hastings, last night, gave a new character to the ancient residence of the Grand Masters. They seemed to look out from their pictures with surprise upon what was going on ; and to think, in spite of the many changes which the island had witnessed, that *this* was the most *outré* of all ! Peradventure, they were right ; but it was, nevertheless, an imposing scene. Monks of the

Order of St. Dominic were moving about in the peculiar dresses of their caste; and almost brought to life again departed ages. The scarlet uniforms of the military, the " waving plumes," the fair smiling faces which converted the apartments of the palace " into a firmament glistered with breathing stars," were all of them objects upon which a sage might have looked with satisfaction, though it were tinctured with regret : for he might have asked *why* they were assembled——to what profitable end ? Were they better, or were they happier ? In all probability, he would have thought *not !* And he might have lifted up the veil of futurity, and beheld all these animated and animating objects mingled with the dust ; loathsome relics of mortality——things that the heart sickens to contemplate. But for all that, one who is *not a sage,*——one who takes matters just as he finds them, would have been pleased with the scene before him. A philanthropist would have hoped that they were the happier, and a philanthropic moralist, that they were the better. An enthusiast would have believed it at once ; and the satiated man of the world, whilst he constrained his features to return the

smile which saluted them, would pronounce a
bitter curse upon the heartlessness of refined
society, and the mockery of worldly pleasure!
How far any, or all of these, are constituent
parts of the *man of wisdom;* let those answer
who will.

CHAPTER IX.

FRIDAY, 8*th April.*—I mentioned, a few days ago, the trial of certain Greeks, for piracy and murder. The whole statement of this extraordinary case has been published by authority in the Government Gazette. It is, on a variety of accounts, so extremely interesting, it will serve to illustrate, in so many ways, the character of certain portions of Grecian warfare, and solve so many problematical circumstances which may hereafter appear in this Journal, that I transcribe it without scruple, taking the liberty at the same time to correct some grammatical inaccuracies, and involutions of phrase.

" It will be recollected that *Salvatore Fernandez,* (who was considered as the original planner of the piracy committed on board the Maltese brig *La Speranza,* of which five of his companions have been found guilty, after a most deliberate investigation at the late Admiralty Sessions), hung himself in prison, in August last. He had, however, made a confession, before the magistrate for the Ports. This document was not produced at the trial, as it was considered not legally available in proof of the guilt of his confederates. Still it is supposed to contain the fullest and most circumstantial account of this truly horrible transaction. We therefore give it at length.

" *Confession, taken through the medium of a sworn interpreter.*

" ' On the 1st September last, Captain Giovanni Mavromicali wrote to me a letter from Zimova in Maina, addressed to me at Calamata, requesting that I would go there and enter on board his privateer. I accordingly went to Zimova; and on my arrival, Captain Mavromicali told me to go on board, as he was ready to proceed on a cruize off Scondra or in the Levant; but we did not sail for about thirty-five days afterwards. Captain Mavromicali is brother of the general commanding that district, Petro Bey. The privateer was a mistico, the name of which I do

not remember, and commanded by Captain
Hadgi Panajotti, who is related to Captain
Mavromicali and Petro Bey. On the day following my arrival at Zimova, Captain Giovanni
invited me to come and dine with him at his
house, at twelve o'clock. The first conversation that took place between us, was about
some prizes Captain Mavromicali had tried to
capture at Piscardo, in Cephalonia, but he had
been prevented by the English; these were two
Turkish vessels, one of them a trabaccolo and
the other a brig. He said, the English loved
the Turks more than those who were Christians,
and that, if when we were cruizing I should
fall in with any English, Imperial, French, or
other vessels, I must do my duty by killing
the people whenever I should find cash on
board, and sink the vessels. I was engaged to
be superintendent over the crew, being an old
man; but I was not an officer, though Captain
Mavromicali promised I should live in the
cabin with the captain and officers; but being
a bad man, he has put me down as second
captain. When the before-mentioned conversation took place, I answered, that I would not
go on board his vessel being such a man as he

was. Captain Mavromicali replied, he thought I was a different character than I appeared to be, and that he was only joking with me ; and he would not act in the manner he had said.

" ' On the following day, early in the morning, there was a boat ready to sail for Calamata, in which I applied for a passage, as I wished to return to Calamata. I was on board of the Mistico, and the boat came alongside to take me off. Captain Mavromicali seeing this, and supposing I was going to embark in the boat, called out to me from the shore, and asked why I was going away without first informing him. He then desired me to come on shore, as he wanted to give me a letter for Mr. Giacomo Cornelio, at Calamata ; and besides the letter, he would give me an order upon him for six dollars, which was one month's salary ; I accordingly went on shore, and took from him the letter and order for six dollars, and then went into the boat, and proceeded with it to Calamata, leaving the Mistico at Zimova. We arrived at Calamata on the following day, where on my arrival I delivered to Mr. Cornelio the letter and order ; and, according to the latter, I received from him the six

dollars. After this I went to my house at Calamata, where I remained quiet during five days;
after which the British Vice Consul of Arcadia
came to Calamata: his name was Anastasachi
Pasqualigo; I met him soon after, and he saluted me. After this he came to my house to
take his coffee and make his compliments to me
according to the custom of the Greeks. I then
told him that I was about to reveal a matter
of great consequence—a plot that was forming;
but that I wished he would not mention my
name, fearing I might lose my life. The Vice
Consul then asked me who were the persons
that were intending to execute the plot I hinted
at. I answered, that ' our superiors of this
place and those of Zimova, were the persons.'
I said this, because the Governor of Calamata
was brother of Captain Mavromicali and Petro
Bey. The governor's name is Costantino
Mavromicali. The Vice Consul asked me if
the plot was to be executed against British
subjects, or any other foreigners: I answered
him, ' against all the world, provided money
was on board.' The Vice Consul then told me
he was going to Tripolitza, thence to Arcadia,
and thence to Navarino; and that if any thing

should occur, I was to come to him at the
latter place ; and should any vessel be captured, any money taken, the crew killed, or
the vessel sunk, I was to put all the papers of
the prize or prizes in my breast at the first
place we should arrive at, and come with them
to him at Navarino.   He advised me to go on
board of the Mistico ; it would be better, because should any thing happen at sea I could
discover it.   After this conversation, I remained forty-five days at Calamata ; and after
that time the Mistico arrived there from
Zimova.   On her arrival, the Mistico fired a
salute of ten guns in compliment to the captain's brother, the governor.   The governor of
Calamata ordered me to go that evening on
board of the Mistico, because on the next
morning early she was to take troops on board,
and convey them to Coron, for the purpose of
attacking the castle at that place.——I accordingly embarked ; and on the next morning
seventy soldiers were taken on board.   The
Mistico then set sail, but on account of bad
weather, we put into Petatidi, where the
soldiers were landed, and Captain Panajotti
went along with them, from mere curiosity, to

witness the attack on the castle of Coron. On the next day he returned, and told the crew, that as the castle would not be attacked for five or six days, there was no occasion to remain; we therefore went to Armiro. After the six days the Greeks attacked the castle, when we proceeded to Coron near the castle, to see if it had been captured. On our arrival, we perceived that the Greeks had lost the battle; so we left and returned to Armiro. Two days after, the weather being fine, we set sail from Armiro, bound to Coron, to bring back the General of the Greek troops, Captain Costantino Mavromicali, the governor of Calamata, and the troops that had been embarked in the Mistico. The Mistico returned with them to Armiro, which is the port of Calamata. Another brother of Captain Costantino, Captain Antonachi, wrote a letter from Coron to his brother, and sent it to him at Armiro; in consequence of which letter Captain Costantino called me and the captain of the Mistico, and shewing us the letter, desired us to proceed immediately to Coron, as a vessel with provisions had arrived there to succour the Turks in the castle.

" ' We accordingly, on the same evening, set sail for Coron, where we came to anchor, close to Vunaria. On the next morning Capt. Panajotti immediately went on shore to speak to Captain Antonachi, who was in camp there. At twelve o'clock he returned on board, and told the whole of the crew that the order was, should a vessel be captured near the castle, she and her cargo would be condemned, be her flag what it might. After this Captain Panajotti brought upon deck an image of the Virgin Mary; and calling all the crew, desired them to take an oath, that they would willingly consent to kill the crew of that vessel, of whatever nation she might be—English, Imperial, French, or any other; and further, that they would kill the crew, sink the vessel, and take from her whatever they might find on board. The whole of the crew then took the oath. I was the last one, I took the oath because I could not help it. The captain further said to the crew, ' you know our conditions are these: that four shares of the prize will belong to the four captains on shore;' namely, Captain Costantino Mavromicali, governor of Calamata; Captain Giovanni Mavromicali, his brother, generally called Cazzi;

Captain Kristair, whose son intended to marry the daughter of Captain Cazzi, brother of Petro Bey; and the fourth, Mr. Giacomo Cornelio, a native of Zante, residing at Calamata, and *one of the first nobles of Zante.* To which four persons were likewise to be paid four thousand piastres for expences of the Mistico already incurred, which were first to be deducted from the whole proceeds; and the remaining proceeds of the prize, either money or any thing else, were to be divided; namely, one half to the four persons before named, who were the sole owners of the Mistico, and the other half to the crew; but out of this latter half, the owners were to be paid the four shares before stated. At this time, when Captain Panajotti was explaining the business to the crew, I remained silent, sitting upon a gun, reflecting seriously, and much displeased. The captain, seeing me in this humour, said to me, ' what is the matter with you; what are you thinking about?' I replied, ' I am sure that vessel is an English one; we shall displease the English, and should we fall in with an English frigate, she will sink us.' The captain answered, addressing himself to all the crew: ' If the

English have a good fleet, we have our mountains, which are much stronger than their men
of war.' After this, the captain took me down
into the cabin, and shewed me a letter signed
by the four persons before mentioned ; which
letter stated, ' *Don't fear any thing ; do what
you can, and you shall be defended by us, all
in our power.*'

" ' After this we set sail, and went near to
the vessel anchored by the castle of Coron, and
fired two guns at her. At the same time the
castle fired a gun at the Mistico, and the vessel
moved nearer to the shore, and under the protection of the castle ; so we quitted the place,
and steered towards Cape Gallo, where we perceived three vessels sailing eastward. The captain said we had better go and visit them. And
we pursued them for three hours, but could
not come up with them ; part of the crew said
we had better abandon the chase, and return
to Coron, as the vessel there might set sail.
We accordingly returned, and during the remainder of that and the following day we
cruised about.

" ' On the evening of the latter day, three
hours after sun-set, we fell in with the Maltese

vessel, named *La Speranza*; I think that was her name, commanded by Captain Francisco Gristi. We hailed her: Captain Mari, a Cephaloniote, hailed her with a speaking-trumpet, and desired the captain to come on board in his boat, and bring his papers with him. The vessel then let a boat down, into which the Maltese captain, a Greek passenger, and two seamen, four in all, embarked. I should have stated, that when the captain of the Mistico ordered the Maltese brig to be hailed, I asked him for what reason he ordered the captain to come on board? Captain Panajotti replied, he wanted to see if there were any Turks on board, or papers for Constantinople. I replied, ' you must consider, that the vessel and her master are Maltese, and belonging to my own country, and if you attempt to molest her, from friends that we now are, we shall become enemies.' Captain Panajotti answered, ' the English took from me a million, at Piscardo, and I will take from them much more; if you speak any more, I'll serve you the same as I intend to do the Maltese.' Saying this, he knocked me down ; my head struck on the nail of a gun, and made a wound. Afterwards the brig's boat came alongside, with the four persons I had before mentioned. They were called upon the Mistico's deck, when the Maltese captain and the Greek passenger were sent down into the cabin, and the two seamen were sent into the hold. The hands and legs of the Maltese captain and Greek passenger were tied, — the same was done to the two seamen. Immediately after Captain Panajotti ordered thirteen of the Mistico's crew to go on board of the Maltese brig. The names of some of them I recollect; these were Elia, nephew of Petro Bey; Capt. Mari, the Cephaloniote; Giorgi the Nostromo, a Spetziote; the son of Captain Panajotti, Cristodulo; Costantino, a Previsan; Mosca, a Corfiote; Pano, a Previsan, who is one of those in custody; Spiro, a Calavritan, another of those in custody; and Costantino di Giorgio, a Spetziote, the boy now in custody. I do not recollect the names of the others. I now remember another was Anagnosti, the brother-in-law of Captain Panajotti; and another named Nicola Lagonica, nephew of the captain; and another named Scartato, a Zantiote. They were

all well armed with pistols, and large knives
called attaghani. It was moon-light, and almost calm.

" ' As soon as they got on board of the
Maltese brig, Anagnosti went to the poop of
the brig and hailed Captain Panajotti, saying
to him, ' ask the Maltese captain where the
key of his chest is to be found.' Captain
Panajotti answered, that the key was in a
small drawer in the cabin, where the Maltese
captain slept. The two vessels were very close
to each other. Anagnosti, about three-quarters
of an hour after, came again to the poop of
the brig, and spoke to Captain Panajotti in
the Albanese language, which I do not understand. Immediately after this I heard three
pistol-shots fired ; after which Capt. Panajotti
ordered the crew of the Mistico that remained
on board to go alongside and board the brig.
The whole of the crew then went on board of
the prize ; and began to take out of her chests
belonging to the captain and crew, sails, ropes,
and many other things, which they put into
the Mistico. An hour after the brig had been
boarded, Captain Panajotti ordered all the
people to return to the Mistico, except the

thirteen persons who were first sent on board.
I and five or six others did not board the brig:
we remained in the Mistico to receive the
things from her. Captain Panajotti ordered
ten muskets to be given to the thirteen hands
on board the brig, to defend themselves with.
The vessels then separated; this was about
midnight. The Mistico steered towards Vunaria, and the prize towards Capo Grosso. On
our way towards Vunaria, Captain Panajotti
ordered the deck to be cleared of the things
taken out of the brig. After this was done,
he ordered the crew to put the two Maltese
seamen to death. They were then brought on
deck and carried to the forecastle, and there
put to death; but in what manner I cannot
say, as I was astern on the poop, and did not
see them. When this was done, the Greek
passenger was brought upon deck, and Captain
Panajotti asked him what money he possessed.
The passenger replied, he had only thirty dollars. The Greek said to the Captain, 'don't
put me to death, because I am a Christian,
like you; you are quite right to kill the Maltese dogs,—those you have killed,—because
they dont like us at all.' Upon this, Captain

Panajotti said, 'take this man also forward,' meaning to say that he was to be put to death with the others. After this, Captain Panajotti went astern, and called to Gregorio, (one of those now in custody), who was in the cabin, and had tied the Maltese captain and Greek passenger, and stood guard over them. He desired him to bring the Maltese captain upon deck; which he did, and brought him to the middle of the vessel. At this time Captain Panajotti asked the Maltese captain what sum of money he had in his chest. He answered him, he had one thousand seven hundred and seventy dollars. Immediately after Captain Panajotti said, 'take this man also forward with the others.' At this time he asked Athanasi, the cook, where he had put the rope he had given to him from the Maltese vessel. The cook immediately brought the rope, and gave it to Captain Panajotti, who cut it into four pieces, and gave them to the cook, saying to him, 'go forward, and tell the people to put the dead bodies into four bags. Put some ballast into them, and tie them with the four pieces of rope, and throw them overboard.' I did not see either of the four put to death, but

I heard every thing. I was in such bad humour, I would not see any thing; and vexed as I was, I took my capote, and remained on the poop. I do not know if either or all of the four prisoners said any thing. I was alarmed, and wounded in the head, when the captain knocked me down. I tied my head with a handkerchief; the wound is perfectly healed, but can be seen.

" ' After this the Mistico steered for Vunaria; where, having arrived, Captain Panajotti ordered two persons to go on shore. One of them was named Panajotti Gianni, and the other Anagnosti, the brother-in-law of the captain, who came on board from the Maltese brig before we parted from her. He was replaced by another man of the same name. The two persons sent on shore did not return on board. At day-light the next morning, the Mistico steered in the direction of the prize, to look after her. We remained at sea all the day. At mid-day we perceived the prize, and about sun-set we came near to her, when Captain Panajotti hailed the Nostromo, and asked him if he was ready. The Nostromo replied ' We are ready.' Then Captain Panajotti or-

10

dered the Mistico's boat to go alongside of the prize, and bring the people back. The boat went accordingly and returned again with two or more cases of rosolio, some sails and wearing apparel ; also four or five pieces of calico, a bale of Maltese brown nankeens and some red handkerchiefs. The boat after discharging these articles returned again to the prize and brought a further quantity of them, compasses, sails, the ship's bell, plates, knives and forks, and other articles. The boat returned again to the prize and brought back part of the people who were on board ; and her boat brought the remainder of the thirteen who took charge of her. When they returned Captain Panajotti asked them if they had prepared the brig for sinking. They replied all was well done, and that she would soon go down. Captain Panajotti then asked them what they had done with the crew of the brig who remained on board. Three of them, namely, Pano Previsiano, Costantino Calavritano, (both of them in custody) and the third, Scartato, replied, ' We put them to death at twelve o'clock to-day.' The captain asked if any of the Maltese had been killed by the pistols they heard fired. They answered no—

but two of them had been wounded, and the others concealed themselves under the deck. They said they had found on board seven of the crew, whom they had put to death with pistols and with knives. I cannot say if they made any resistance. Elia, nephew of Petro Bey, was wounded in the head. He said it was by a blow given him with a piece of wood by one of the Maltese. He said to me at the same time, that for that wound in his head my head should pay for it, because he had received it from a Maltese like me. Captain Panajotti then asked what had become of the murdered bodies. They answered they had taken the whole of them down into the store or steward's room. The captain then enquired if they had fastened down the hatchways. They replied, ' Yes, perfectly well.' About half an hour after this the prize went down.

" ' On the following morning the captain ordered all the clothes which were in the chests of the seamen of the Maltese brig to be divided. Half of the whole was set apart for the owners of the Mistico ; and the other half distributed in proportions. They offered to me three shirts, two jackets, and some other things, but I refused to accept any of them, saying, ' My heart does not even wish to look at these clothes.' From the Maltese captain's chests there were taken some Spanish dollars : they amounted to seventeen hundred and seventy. This cash was not divided until after our arrival at Armiro. There were also twelve Greek capoti of a black colour, not new, which were distributed to those who first boarded the brig. Two of them are now in the possession of two of the prisoners in custody, namely, Pano Previsano and the boy Costantino. They have also each of them a sash, some shirts, and each a black cap common in Malta. The whole of the prisoners now in custody have each in their possession some of the clothes that were taken from the Maltese brig. On our arrival at Armiro, according to the order I had received, as I said before, from the British Vice Consul, when the chest of the Maltese captain was opened (it was the last one opened), I was very attentive to get hold of his papers ; so perceiving a tin case, I took hold of it, and from it withdrew three papers, namely, the passport, the patent, and muster roll. I took possession of these papers, and concealed them

under my sash.   In the captain's chest there
were found a gold repeater, two seals, and a gold
watch-key; four gold rings with small diamonds; a shirt-pin with a small diamond, a
small gold cross with topazes, and a gold cord.
From the chests of the seamen there were taken
three silver watches, in addition to their wearing apparel.   Captain Panajotti ordered his
son, in whose possession those articles were, to
bring the money on deck to be divided, which
was brought up accordingly. The captain then
ordered the four thousand piastres for the expences of the Mistico to be first deducted.
Upon this a dispute arose: some of the crew
said they would not consent to it, and others
would not consent that the four owners should
take four shares of the half which was to belong to the crew.   About these they had a long
dispute.   At last they agreed, that instead of
four, the owners should only have two thousand
piastres for the vessel's expences. The other
two thousand were to remain on board for the
expences of the next cruize. The four shares
before mentioned were given up to the owners.
The remainder of the money was distributed,
as follows : forty-five dollars to each of the

11

thirteen who boarded the Maltese brig, and
twenty dollars to all the others. I do not
know what amount was taken by the captain
and the other officers; because my mind was
wholly bent upon saving the ship's papers and
delivering them into the hands of the British
Vice Consul Pasqualigo. The captain offered,
and gave me, twenty-three dollars; telling me
to take them for the present, and that the next
voyage I should have much more. I refused
to accept the twenty-three dollars; but the
captain told me he would not allow me to go
on shore if I did not take them, so I was compelled to take them. Some of the things were
put up at auction. The captain purchased the
gold repeater and the four rings. I do not
know what he paid for them, as I was at the
helm. He came to me and said, that as he
had purchased the gold watch and the rings,
he did not like to appear to buy any more
things, and requested that I would purchase
for him the gold cross with topazes, as he
wished to give it to his daughter. I accordingly complied with his request, and went and
offered six dollars for it; when the captain
said, " Well, it is for you;"—when in fact I

purchased it for him. Half an hour after I delivered the cross to the captain. Of the silver watches, the spy Gregorio took one I think, for about eighty piastres; another was taken by a Mainote whose name I do not know, and the third was taken by Spiro Calavritino, who is in custody. The division and auction took place at sea. The money was divided in the cabin, on the morning after our arrival at Armiro, which took place two hours after sun-set. The division of the clothes and the auction took place in midships an hour after I consented to receive the twenty-three dollars, which were forced upon me. At twelve o'clock I jumped into the Mistico's boat, and attempted to go on shore. The captain told me to stop a moment, and said 'I wish to go with you on shore.' I waited some time in the boat, and the captain went into the cabin, and I think brought with him the gold repeater, the four rings, with all the money belonging to him, and to the owners of the Mistico, and carried them to the house of the Governor of Calamata, Captain Costantino Mavromicali.

" ' When we reached the shore Captain Pa-

CONFESSION OF A GREEK PIRATE.

najotti and I each took a horse and proceeded together to Calamata. Before I left the Mistico, I sent Strati, one of the prisoners now in custody, on shore, to go to Calamata and bring me a horse to Armiro. The horse which the captain rode belonged to Armiro, Strati having sent only one : he remained at Calamata. We, that is, the captain and myself, arrived at Calamata two hours before sun-set. I went to my own house, and delivered the ship's papers, which I had concealed, to my wife. An hour after this, namely, an hour after sun-set, the nephew of the governor, Elia Cazzacho met me at the market. As soon as he saw me, he seized hold of me, and said that the crew of the Mistico had sent notice to Captain Panajotti that I had taken the ship's papers; and that Captain Panajotti having applied to the governor, he (Elia) had come to arrest me. He then conveyed me to the house of Captain Costantino, the governor. As soon as I arrived there the governor ordered me to be tied, and diligent search made about my person for the papers : and not finding any thing, except the twenty-three dollars before mentioned, Elia went to my house and asked my wife where the papers were which she had received from me. She, not knowing any thing of what had happened to me, delivered them to him. When Elia returned with the papers to the house of the governor, the governor said to me, 'You are a damned dirty dog for having stolen these papers; you must have had a bad intention.' I replied, 'I took the papers to preserve them, and not with the bad intention which you say.' Notwithstanding this I was put into a room of the governor's house, where (in the same room) six men were placed as a guard over me. I remained there during that night; and on the following morning a declaration was presented to me to sign. I said I would not sign it until its contents were explained to me. The governor replied 'Very well, I'll read it to you; and then you'll sign it.' On reading over this paper I found the tenor of it to be this:—That five miles off Coron the Mistico perceived a brig at sea,—the Mistico fired a musket for the brig to lay to,—the brig then fired a gun, and the shot from it killed two persons on board the Mistico; so the privateer answered with a shot: and soon after, the brig was seen sinking, and immediately went to the bottom.—

Upon this being read to me, I refused to sign it, saying it was not the truth, and I would never consent; but that they might get it signed by the captain of the Mistico and other persons of her crew. In consequence of this refusal, I was tied with my hands between my legs; and a stone weighing thirty pounds was put on my breast. Placing a pistol to my head, Elia Cazzacho told me, that if I did not consent to sign the paper he would put me to death. I said 'Take off the stone and I will sign it.' After this, as I cannot read or write, they told me to make the sign of the cross,—which I complied with in the presence of a Greek priest and three gentlemen of Calamata, as witnesses to my mark. One of the three latter is a relation of Petro Bey, and his christian-name Theodosio; the second is named, I think, Giovanni Costantinachi; the name of the third I do not recollect.—The Greek priest was named, I think, Papa Athanasi. As soon as I had put my mark, Elia said, ' In consequence of this you will be hanged at Zante or at Malta.' Notwithstanding that I had consented to sign the declaration, I was kept a prisoner in the same room for the space of four

days.   After which I saw pass by the house,
the nostromo of the Mistico and four other of
her crew, namely, Costantine the boy, Spiro
Calavritino, Pano Previsano, and Athanasi
Mosconissiote; which last four are now in custody. I heard that these five had been carried
to the house of the bishop.   I forgot to mention, that another of those in custody, named
Strati Aivaliote, was arrested on the same day
as myself, and brought prisoner to the same
room.   On the following day I and Strati were
conveyed to another house, where we found
the other five, with whom we were confined in
the same room.   This house belonged to my
mother-in-law, which was taken from her by
force; and she attempted to set fire to it.
Twelve or thirteen days after the acting British
Vice Consul of Calamata, Ignazio Giovanni
Hadgi Yanuli, came into the house and went
up stairs.   (We were confined on the ground
floor.)   They sent for the nostromo, who went
to them accordingly; and when he was entering the room where they were I heard the acting British Vice Consul say to him, if he wished
to get his liberty he must sign the attestation
that had been signed by Gregorio.   The nos-

tromo replied he would not sign it until he had his liberty. Soon after, the other four who were brought with the nostromo were sent for up stairs, the nostromo remaining there also. The acting British Vice Consul said the same to them, namely, that upon their signing the attestation they should be set at liberty:—so they all five signed the paper; the whole of them came down stairs; when I asked them what they had been doing, they told me nothing at all. About five or six days after, the adjutant of the governor, accompanied by Cazzacho, the nephew, and Giorgio Mavromicali, the son of Petro Bey, came to the house, and sent for the nostromo; and soon after I heard that he had run away. About the same time two persons entered our prison with sticks in their hands, and began to beat all of us, under the pretence that we knew where he was gone, and that we were privy to his escape. On the next day they sent the attestations signed by us to Anastasachi Pasqualigo, the British Vice Consul at Arcadia. In consequence of this Mr. Pasqualigo wrote a letter to the acting British Vice Consul at Calamata, stating that the facts could not be as they had been repre-

sented to him, because he had heard of them
two months before.   The acting British Vice
Consul at Calamata having received this letter
from Mr. Pasqualigo, immediately went to
Captain Costantino to inform him of its contents; and Captain Costantino said to him,
' We had better write another letter to him,
requesting him not to discover us, he being a
Greek and a Christian." On the next day
they wrote a letter to him, and sent a present
to him of honey loaded on four mules, six antique stones, and the gold repeater of the deceased Maltese captain ; desiring him to be so
kind as to receive them as a little proof of their
regard, and as a recompence for the assistance
they hoped to receive from him.   After being
confined thirty-six or thirty-seven days a British frigate arrived, and on the same day in
the afternoon we were conveyed on board.

" ' The frigate carried us to Zante, where I
was examined, but what I said I do not recollect, having been frequently interrupted, and
not permitted to speak. On board the Mistico
I sometimes wore an European and sometimes
a Greek dress, the same as is worn at Calamata. The deceased captain and the Greek

passenger, when brought down into the cabin, were tied by Gregorio, the spy. I do not know who tied the hands of the two seamen. The Maltese brig arrived at Calamata when I was at Ignocastro. On my return I found her lying there. I had known her captain, Francesco Gristi, on a previous voyage to Calamata a year before. I was requested by him to purchase some figs for him, which I did—about twenty or twenty-five cantars, perhaps more. I am married to a native of Calamata, she was living there when I left it. I have been absent from Malta about twelve years, but came to Malta during the plague to settle some accounts. I was previously married in Malta to a native woman, but left her as she proved a woman of bad character. On board the Mistico I sometimes lived in the cabin and sometimes messed with the crew. My wages were six dollars per month. When I quitted the Mistico for the last time I left Gregorio on board. The crew of the Mistico was composed of thirty-five or thirty-six persons in all. I brought the letter which I had received from Captain Giovanni Mavromicali, dated 1st of September, on board the frigate; but lost it

there.   The letter now exhibited to me is one
which I received from the same person; and
is, I think, dated in January.   It desired me
to come to Zimova, and embark on board the
Mistico. I went there, and afterwards returned
to Calamata; as the voyage was defeated
through the soldiers she was to convey from
Armiro to the attack of the Castle at Coron.
I have known Gregorio Mavrichi, who is in
custody, about six months.   I heard on board
that he was a Mainote.   He was first gunner
of the two large guns which were at the forecastle of the Mistico.

 " ' Of the various wearing apparel now shown
to me in court, I know that a white shirt which
was in the possession of Spiro Calavritano (one
of the prisoners in custody) was taken from the
Maltese brig.   The Greek capote, the red sash,
and the dark-coloured handkerchief, were in
possession of Pano Previsano, (also in custody);
and were likewise taken from the Maltese brig.
The capote now shown to me was in the possession of Costantino the boy (who is in custody);
it was taken from the Maltese brig.   The shirt
and the red sash, now produced, were in the
possession of Strati Aivalioti, and were taken

from the Maltese brig. The quilted coverlid, and I believe the white shirt, were in the possession of Gregorio, (who is in custody) ; and they were both taken from the Maltese brig. Of the bundle now shown to me, the blue cloth jacket I received at Calamata from Signor Giovanni Coronetopulo ; the coloured waistcoat I brought from my house at Calamata ; and the blue striped shirt was given to me by the government at Zante. As for the linen shirt and the coloured handkerchief, I do not know to whom they belong. The sash shawl, which I have now upon my person, I purchased at Calamata, about twelve months ago, from a sailor of a Maltese bombard, commanded by Captain Vincenzo Cachia : the sailor is named Pasquale San Martino. The two striped jackets or waistcoats were taken from the Maltese brig. One of them was in the possession of Costantino, the boy in custody ; and the other was in the possession of Athanasi Misconissiote, the cook on board the Mistico, and now in custody. I know these two jackets were taken from the Maltese brig, because such are never worn by Greeks. I gave to Atanasio Mosconissiote, one of the prisoners, a white calico shirt ; it

was very old; and he tore it up to put round
the iron fetters which were on his legs. I gave
the shirt to him at Zante; and he gave me
another white shirt, one of three in his possession, which had been taken from the Maltese
brig. It ought to be at the prison, as I washed
it the day before yesterday; and it ought to be
clean.

" ' I confirm this my voluntary confession;
the same having been read to me word for
word in the Greek language, by the sworn interpreter; and not knowing how to write, I
make the sign of the cross.'

his

(Signed)   " ' Salvadore ✝ Fernandes,
mark.

" ' Giuseppe Coen, Sworn Interpreter.

" ' This confession taken by me,
  and signed in my presence, this
  7th day of July, 1824.
    " ' James Calvert,
Acting Magistrate for the Ports.' "

" His Excellency the Governor has been since
pleased to commute the sentence of death, in
consequence of the prisoners having been recommended to mercy by the jury, on the

ground that they seem to have been rather
blind instruments in the hands of others, than
the planners of the piracy. *Pano Cavani,
Strati Cojungi,* and *Spiridion di Giorgio Lico,*
are to be transported for the period of their
natural lives ; and *Costantino Marini Gior-
ghizza* and *Atanasio Silvriano,* for fourteen
years, to such place as His Majesty may please
to direct.

" By the arrival of His Majesty's transport
Maria, from Cephalonia and Zante, we are
informed, that the Turkish fleet, consisting of
eleven ships of war, entered the Gulf of Patrass
on the 27th ultimo, convoying many Austrian
vessels, laden with provisions and ammunition,
which had been detained at Zante by the
Greek blockade.

" The *Messolongi Gazette* of 12th February,
announces the appointment of a commission of
nine members for the trial of those chiefs who
have lately acted against the Provisional Government. The only other intelligence is a confirmation of the active preparations, particularly in Albania, for the ensuing campaign.
The Albanese, it is thought, will not delay
their invasion of the Plains of the Peloponesus

until June and July, as has been hitherto their practice."

Tuesday, 12th April. — Yesterday, Lady Neale contrived a *pic-nic* party to Boschetto, a sort of country house, or " bosky bourne," anciently belonging to the Grand Masters. It is a handsome square building, flanked by towers of the same character. A deep fosse surrounds it ; but otherwise it does not discover any sign of having been used as a place of defence. Its elevation is, perhaps, the most considerable in the island; and affords a fine prospect of much the largest portion of the territory, including the Island of Gozo, which may be easily distinguished. Its internal condition is now the most desolate imaginable; the painting is defaced upon the walls, and both the windows and the doors are demolished. The sleeping apartment of the Grand Masters alone, (their bed is colder now, and their sleep sounder than it was!) has a fireplace ; and a miserable recess, above which a Maltese cross is blazoned, formed the place of their occasional repose. One of the towers supplied a small dressing-room.

At the foot of the castle is a valley, remarkable for the grove of orange trees, which is almost the only specimen of that description of fertility which Malta displays. At all events, it is certainly the most extensive : and, at this season of the year, when the cultivated land puts on its fairest aspect, the appearance of this " green spot," amid the barrenness and aridness of all around, is exceedingly striking and agreeable. A stream of water gushes through it amid an unusual luxuriance of olive trees. Here the bramble flourishes ; of which a young English lady (to whom I allude with sincere and merited respect,) averred that of all other things it soonest brought back to her recollection the feelings of early youth, and the beauties of her native land. A leaf or a flower might have done the same ; but these were common objects—common as men's faces, and stood not alone, like the solitary bramble, in the most retired and verdant portion of the island ; almost beautiful from its rarity, and loved for its affinity with something beloved ! And she broke off two or three branches of the hallowed bramble;—this was for one friend, and that was for another. " There was——— poor fellow ! he was indisposed, and should

Have something to comfort him,—give him
this;" so she sent him a thorn! Strange
power of association! and stranger still the
power of natural sentiments developed in a
natural manner! I never thought so well of the
human heart, as I did upon this occasion.

We were a party of about thirty; and we
eat, and drank, and danced, and laughed—
" *as though the earth contained no tomb;*"
and as though one painful reflection should
never again start up into anxious life. We
had bade farewell to sorrow; and we hoped,
perhaps, to meet with her no more! But the
vulture will not be driven wholly from the
prey. The shout of merriment may raise her
a moment upon the wing, but she descends
again with redoubled eagerness and fury. It
is, after hours of high-strained hilarity, that
solicitude is experienced the most.

As I rode to the theatre of action, being
somewhat puzzled about the way, I put my
head to a grated window that I passed, and
was saluted with a most alarmingly sonorous
" *viva!*" Out came " a tall thin gentleman,"
equipped very much like a cook: his hair was
of an intense black, plaited and 'tied' behind

his head *en queue.* He had a bustling, self-
complacent mien, and spoke broken unintelli-
gible English; but his prompt and decisive manner plainly indicated that he himself held another estimate of its worth. I enquired the way:
" yes," he answered—" the way is. You must
ask. Me tell you; go—ask." I interrupted
my informant with something of impatience,
but before I could speak, he burst forth with
" welcome !"—as though he supposed I was
expressing my gratitude—" the way is. You
go—and ask." I thought it time; so I rode
forward, followed, on a full trot, by the com-
municative " tall thin gentleman," whose mel-
low tones and choice phraseology I heard behind me for nearly five minutes after I had
left him. About half the distance, (having
been previously joined by two friends,) we rode
on at a brisk canter in order to avoid a shower
of rain, which threatened to put an end to
the pleasure of our excursion, and overtook a
middle-aged monk, of a most dingy complexion, mounted on a mule, or rather on the
well-filled panniers which his mule carried. We
passed rapidly on; but our monk, whom some
fiend inspired with an ambition to " witch

the world with noble horsemanship," stuck his heels into " Muley Hassan." His long-eared friend not understanding the laudable intention, or not relishing the experiment, began to caper most asininely; the paniers turned round, and the whole machinery of the poor ascetic turned with them. He clung with such an air of vexation, breaking from beneath his huge three-cornered hat, to the neck of the mule, and twined his long black legs so awkwardly around it, that a more ridiculous picture never met the visual ken of a laughter-loving spirit. We drew up our steeds and saluted him ; but whether he thought that it was done maliciously, or that he was overwhelmed with confusion at the undignified figure he had cut, true it is, that he replied, by an affected nod, which added yet more strikingly to the absurd situation in which he was placed, and made it almost impossible to restrain the laugh inspired by the occasion. We presently lost sight of him, no doubt " chewing the cud of sweet and bitter fancy :" —the first, in that he had escaped so well ; and the last, in that he had acquitted himself no better.

We returned to Valetta about nine o'clock, with feelings, I will venture to say, as varied as the hues of a prism; although, perhaps, not *all* so highly coloured. Of the party, were Lord Crofton, whom I cannot but mention with respect; Admiral Sir Harry Neale; and Sir Charles Burrard, whose kindness and good-nature are above comment; Lady Richardson and her daughter, whom I regret that I do not know more of; Miss W. Whitmore, who is one of the " best creatures living;" with sundry other right fair and right fashionable personages, " all honourable," but whom I lament that my present Gazette cannot designate in the full odour of their renown. This arises chiefly from " press of matter," as all the world knows.

Wednesday, 13th April.—" Proud day for Malta this." The colours of the 95th regiment were consecrated by Mr. Le Mesurier, and presented by the Marchioness of Hastings. In the evening a splendid ball was given by the officers, at the Auberge de Provence. A *clerical* gentleman (whose character, alas! will be but little affected by the anecdote!) was so intoxicated on this occasion, as to be

made the subject of the most indecorous exposure. He was crammed into an *empty* claret
hogshead; and, it is said, his chief complaint,
on returning to his senses,—or rather, on
awakening from sleep !—was, its *emptiness !*
He was afterwards (on the same evening too)
conveyed up the chimney; a circumstance
which somebody entitled, " *a new way of re-
novating a black coat.*" The stains communicated by such conduct, are of the deepest
dye; they are the leopard's spots—the Æthio-
pian's darkness ! But though the *person* cannot be cleansed of such impurities, the *church*
might, and ought !

Thursday, 14th April.—In a Latin preface
to a Maltese grammar, published at Rome in
1791, I find certain morsels of biblical cri-
ticism, that are at least curious : I shall, therefore translate them. Speaking of the word
RACA, the writer observes, " interpreters vary
as to the signification of this word. Some de-
duce it from the Greek ῥάκως, a piece of cloth
or rag. Others imagine it only an interjection
expressive of anger; and others supply other
explanations. But the force of this word *raca*
is manifest in the Maltese language ; for it hath

Rik *spittle, saliva,* from a disused radical verb Rak *jrak,* to spit, of which we preserve the enlarged word Rejjak, to stain with spittle. And in this signification of *spittle or saliva,* I suppose the word *raca* to be taken. For instance, ' whoever shall say to his brother *raca,* is in danger of the council.' Matt. v. 22. *That is,* he who shall evince contempt of his brother, by spitting upon him, shall be in danger of the council.

" In like manner MAMMON may be derived from the particle MYN,—*from, or out of;* and MŬNÆ, which properly signifies in Maltese, *whatever is laid up,* viz.; corn, oil, wine, charcoal, wood, branches, and all kind of annual or monthly provisions; in a word, *every thing reposited.* Hence we say, MŬNÆ TAT-TNÂM, *a store of corn;* MŬNÆ TALLAŞAM, *store of meat,* &c. These were the riches of the ancients; such in truth they are, and therefore were so received. As to the particle MYN, *out of,* it adds greater force to the word MŬNÆ; as though you should say, ' I have something *out of,* or *by reason of,* riches'—for riches themselves: ' they are to me *in consequence of* riches,' that is, in the place of them. This mode of speaking is proper and common to the east. And by aid of the Maltese language, very many other words will find a comment."

The author then goes on to notice the derivation of certain Greek words, which he maintains originated in the Phœnician language. "Thus Καδμος, Cadmus, the man so celebrated among the Greeks. Because he first brought letters from Phœnicia into Greece he was called *Cadmus*, either from the Phœnician *Cadm*, (or in Maltese with the Qof*, Cadm,) that is, *one who conveys or carries*, from the radical verb Cadem. Hence our enlarged Caddem jcaddem, *to carry, to bear, to bring to any one*. Or Cadmus may be derived from *Cadim* (with the Qof Cadim) *ancient*. It also signifies *first*, as it does in the Syriac: thus the Greeks, mindful of this renowned person, called him Cadmus—that is, *ancient* or *first*,—because he first brought letters to them.

"Μυστήριον, *mystery*, is rather from μυσ-

* " Qof; epiglotticum, acutum et gutturale, C aut C."

TŬR, *to lie hid*, *to hide*, of Phœnician origin, than from the Greek μὑω, *to shut*. MYSTŬR with us signifies *covered, veiled, that which is hid* or *concealed* ; from *jystor*, to conceal, to cover, &c. which in Hebrew is סתר, *to lie hid*.

" Βάρβαροι, *barbarians*, (vide 28 chap. of the Acts of the Apostles, ver. 1 and 3.) has received various interpretations. The most natural and genuine meaning in this place may, I think, be found by looking to the origin of the expression. *Barbarus* is a word altogether eastern, passed to the Greeks and Latins by the course of time. Originally it signified no more than *a rustic, a husbandman*, or *occupier of a wilderness :* for it is compounded of two words, BAR, the Syriac for a *son*, and BARR, a *plain, field,* or *wood.* Which word (*barr*) remains also in the Maltese tongue. Thus we say, Ħamȳm yl barr, *wood-pigeons*, or *wild doves*, &c. But amongst the orientals it was customary in the formation of adjectives to take the word BAR, *a son*, with another word indicating the adjective. In this manner, to point out a rustic, or inhabitant of the country, they termed him a *son of the plain, son of the country,* which is the proper signification of *barbarus,* from *barbarr,* viz. a farmer or husbandman, &c. Hence is it that St. Luke, when he wished to indicate certain people rude and dwelling in fields, (the Maltese to wit, and their neighbours who inhabited the country and places near the sea, where there are shipwrecks in winter) terms them properly *barbari* or *barbarians.* And indeed, who beside could St. Paul find in the winter season in those dreary places except *sons of the country* —wild people who occupied those parts for the purpose of cultivation and pasture ? Certainly they were not citizens of Medina (Medina anciently was a city of Malta, and this name it retains at present in the Maltese tongue, namely *Mdina,*) who succoured Paul after his shipwreck !——These things, amongst innumerable others, are sufficient to corroborate what we have said of the usefulness and antiquity of the Maltese tongue."

Saturday, 16th April.—Dined at the Palace. Lady Hastings communicated a very interesting account of the mode by which silkworms are cultivated in India; and which her ladyship (with that attention to every practicable scheme of utility which peculiarly

11

marks her character,) has been endeavouring to introduce into Malta. She has also established a school of industry at St. Antonio for Maltese children, though I fear not as yet with that happy result which the importance of the object merits. Indeed nothing of moment was ever brought about instantaneously; and whatever may be done by perseverance and judgment her ladyship's well-directed efforts will accomplish.

CHAPTER X.

SATURDAY, 23d *April.*——To-day the Marquis of Hastings held a levee; a dinner and ball followed. On Tuesday the Cambrian is to convey his lordship and family to Nice, on their way to England.

Monday, 25th April.——The Marchioness was employed this morning in distributing prizes to the children of the Maltese school established under her ladyship's directions. A variety of articles fabricated by the industry of the English ladies resident in Malta were sold in support of it. The Hon. Mrs. Gardener and the members of her amiable family deserve an especial note of applause on this occasion; not only for the assiduity with which they laboured in providing articles for the sale, but also for their exertions in rendering it effective. A considerable number of dollars was thus raised in aid of this excellent charity.

Mrs. Jowett, (the wife of the missionary of that name) has been extremely serviceable herein ; indeed, she is spoken of as a person of very superior endowments both of mind and heart.

The children were arranged according to their respective classes in the Albergo de Provence, and examined by Lady Hastings in person. The account which she gave of their progress was gratifying; and I do most sincerely hope that the result will be commensurate with the endeavours and praiseworthy intentions of her ladyship.

The Albergo de Provence I formerly alluded to as the garrison ball-room. As a building it is scarcely worth notice; but many of these knightly residences are of splendid dimensions, and of the most ornate style of architecture.

Tuesday, 26th April.—About six o'clock, P.M. the Marquis of Hastings and the whole of his family came on board the Cambrian, accompanied by his staff, and a large concourse of boats filled with English residents and natives of Malta, whom curiosity and respect had drawn to witness the embarkation. The firing then commenced, and continued, at in-

tervals, till we quitted the harbour. It was
nearly dark when we passed the last battery,
and the vivid flashes of the cannon, as it "spoke
to heaven," produced a fine striking effect.
The Sirocco has since blown, and every appearance indicates a swift and agreeable voyage.

Thursday Morning, 28th April.—A circumstance occurred last night which has created much merriment. In the suite of the
Marchioness was a rubicund complexioned
damsel,—" a fair hot wench in flame-coloured
taffeta," of five and fifty years, peradventure,
(but I am an ill judge of these matters) who
might have been our admiral, for she " bore
the lantern in her poop—but it was in the nose
of her." She was the lady " of the burning
lamp," and wandered forth at midnight, bully-
ing the sentry, and making a portentously cla-
mourous appeal to the slumbering organs of the
crew. The Marquis and Marchioness of Hastings were aroused by her vociferations—in
fact, she had surprised and taken possession of
a cabin appropriated to the latter, and perti-
naciously refused to evacuate her post—a military manœuvre which she had no doubt acquired at Malta. The Marquis asserted that

she was *drunk*, and recommended her being put into irons; the Marchioness that she was *mad*, and therefore had more occasion for the doctor, who was sent for accordingly. But the damsel was valorous and resolute: she solemnly protested that she had swallowed *only one bottle of Marcella*, and certain delicate morsels of bread and cheese—("one half-pennyworth of bread to this intolerable deal of sack"—monstrous!) and could not possibly be *drunk*, admitting that she was "*half seas over*;" but a sailor, notorious for his devotion to grog, observing her condition, piously remarked "that he never saw any one half so drunk in his life!" The thing being so, she was ordered to her cabin; and this morning, whether ashamed of the subsequent night's misconduct, or meditating another discussion of the Marcella and cheese, her door was locked, and access unto her shining presence thereby rendered impracticable. Apprehensive of a more fatal catastrophe, a servant was directed to look in at the port-hole which formed the window of her apartment: but all fears were soon dissipated, and she has since *blushed* rather bluer than ordinary!

Communicated this morning with the " *Gannet*," an eighteen gun sloop of war from England.

Thursday Evening.——I am every day called upon to admire the intellectual resources of Lady Hastings. Entering *con amore* into the various scenes to which her high destiny has summoned her, she has been always prepared to meet the exigencies of the period, and to draw from every object a beneficial and edifying character. During her ladyship's residence in India, the zeal with which she prosecuted the most arduous undertakings for the improvement and happiness of the natives, has the testimonial of every traveller of the time ; and I fancy that I am continually discovering some gratifying trait of kindness of heart and strength of intellect. The schools that she established at Barackpore, marked in their progress by the most inveterate prejudices, evince at the same time the spirit with which she commenced, and the humanity and judgment with which she pursued her career. The difficulty of procuring books that the jealousy of the national priesthood would admit, was long a main obstacle to her ladyship's efforts, and this was at length overcome only by giving herself up to the wearisome labour of compiling, or rather of composing books to which no exception could be taken on the score of doctrine. An object of this nature could arise but from the purest and most amiable feelings; and when I observed to her that the undertaking strongly indicated how much she had its welfare at heart, she answered—" that it was true; that a thing of such a description—of such deep and vital interest, must necessarily be had at heart by those who had any heart at all."—I am proud to be the humble instrument of recording these sentiments: I should be proud of it, originating in any class of life, but in a station of such commanding influence—in a sphere where the weight of them is felt as soon as they are uttered, and where a thousand causes contribute to give them an additional efficacy, I am inexpressibly happy! For to say truth, I am something of Sir Edward Coke's opinion, and disposed to think that

" Ubi non est *scientia*, ibi non est *conscentia* ✻."

✻ Institutes, Cap. 63. Fourth Part.

Of the ignorance of the natives of India generally, the Marchioness related a curious anecdote. One of her female attendants absented herself during an eclipse of the moon : on enquiring whither she had been, the woman answered that " *she had been paying the cobler, for that it was quite dark.*" Not perceiving what connection the darkness had with the payment, her ladyship naturally required a solution of the mystery. " Oh !" said the simple creature, " it is a very old story. A long while ago they borrowed nails and a piece of leather of a cobler to nail over the moon. The cobler never was repaid ; so I have been with the rest to pay our share of the money to the priest."——Her ladyship stated herself a good deal amused with the *naïveté* of the girl; and to give her ocular demonstration of the possibility of the moon being eclipsed without being shrouded in a leathern case, she placed herself before a lighted lamp which stood in the apartment, so as to intercept its rays, and then bade her observe how easily the light was diminished and the room obscured. The girl readily comprehended the illustration, (for they are naturally a quick and sensible people) and ran away in great haste and pleasure to communicate the discovery she had made.

Friday, 29th April.—A wet morning reminds me of one or two curious volumes which I picked up during our last visit to Malta. The first is in Latin, and has the following copious title-page. " The Sacred History of the Terrestrial Paradise, and of the most holy State of Innocence : in which is described, I. The Terrestrial Paradise. II. The most blessed Life of Adam and Eve in the Garden. III. The most felicitous State of their Posterity, if their original Uprightness had remained. IV. The Temptation, Sin, Judgment and Punishment of our First Parents. *Lastly,* the wretched Life which for a long Time they dragged on even in sleep. Collected from Scriptures, Councils and Fathers, from Theological, Rabbinical, Historical, Chronological, and Geographical Expositions, &c. By Augustine Inveges, Priest." It was published at Palermo in 1649.

Among other curiosities, it may be thought worthy of mention, that the first age of the world was constantly in the habit of bringing two and three children into the world at a time ; " ob corporis molem, copiosos humores,

et sic providente Deo humani generis multi-
plicationi."—" But how many children were
our first parents blessed with in the whole period of their long life ? This is not quite clear ;
but Epiphanius says twelve sons and two
daughters, Sava and Azura ; the former of
whom was the wife of Cain, and the latter of
Seth. However, Philo Annianus asserts that
they had thirteen sons and five daughters,
whose names he also puts on record. Cedrenus, again, affirms that Adam left thirty-three
sons and twenty-seven daughters, but he cannot give us their names. And if, as Moses
assures us, Adam lived 930, and Eve, as *we*
have shewn above, 940 years, it is not to be
doubted but that, in the course of such a life,
they had a much greater number of both sexes.

" Eve weaned her children when they were
twelve years old ;—so saith Cedrenus. She
also brought forth twins annually, a male and
a female : consequently, in the thirteenth year
of the world, she had twenty-four children,
twelve males and twelve females, to all of whom
it is certain that she gave suck. But how
could a single mother provide for nearly two
dozen babes at the same time, and with her

own milk alone? Verily it is worth a marvel. Salianus however thinks, that for the purpose of supplying nutriment to so many infants, either Eve had a supernatural copiousness of milk, or that it was furnished directly from heaven. Or even that Adam himself, solicitous to obtain milk enough for his offspring, drew it from the udders of his goats and his cattle." —*Here's no foolery!* If human wit cannot employ itself better than in speculations and deductions of such a nature, the sooner mankind convert the world into one huge asylum for lunatics the happier will it be for them. And yet the work in question displays prodigious reading of a particular description, some shrewd conjectures, and not unfrequently a sly smile at the credulity and uncontrolled fancies of others.

> " O the good gods,
> How blind is *pride!* what eagles are we still
> In matters that belong to other men!
> What beetles in our own * !"

But another little volume, at which I have already hinted, is really a very precious relic. It is in French; and professes, in part, to be

* Chapman.—" *All Fools.*"

" An Apology for the grand Work or Elixir of the Philosophers, commonly called THE PHILOSOPHER'S STONE ; wherein the possibility of this work is very clearly demonstrated ; and the gate of true natural philosophy is entirely opened. By Monsieur l'Abbé, D.B." Paris, 1659.

Another part, which is indeed the first, sets forth with " A Treatise on Talismans, or Astral Figures: in which it is shewn, that their effects and admirable virtues are natural. The manner of making them is also discovered, and the mode of using them with profit and singular advantage." Paris, 1671. Third Edition.

And again, " *The Powder of Sympathy Justified.*" Paris, 1671. Third edition.—" Avec privilege du Roy."

The author of this curious production writes with a zeal worthy of a better cause, and is evidently deeply impressed with the conviction of its truth. He complains bitterly of the degraded light in which his favourite studies are considered by the world. " It is now a crime," he exclaims indignantly, " to call oneself a magician ; whereas it was formerly an honour to be one. Celestial astronomy, a science more

worthy of angels than of men, passes only for
an idle dream ; and should we assert, that by
its means we can compose seals, images, characters, and planetary figures, through the aid
of which we are enabled to perform very remarkable and wonderful things, they accuse us
at the same time of having connection with
demons ; and we are constrained to hold our
peace, and bury our light under a bushel, in
order that we may not offend the eyes of the
ignorant, the weak, and the purblind."

After enumerating the various excellencies
of the philosopher's stone, the author proceeds,
" All these marvels, which have charmed the
hearts of sages, have irritated the minds of the
ignorant ; who, being unable to elevate their
thoughts higher than the bound of sense, have
at all times striven to make their elixir of life
pass for some learned trifling—some chimæra—
some delusion. They cannot comprehend how
an elementary substance should cure all sorts of
evils, and even all that species of disorders
which physicians commonly reckon incurable.
They cannot conceive, that, by the use of this
universal medicine, we may wholly preserve
health, and prolong life. They can scarcely

15

persuade themselves that it can act upon all
natural bodies by a means so astonishing.
They know not how to imagine that minerals,
vegetables, and all kinds of animals, find, in
the use of it, deliverance from the evils which
debase them, and the possession of advantages
which elevate them : that lead, tin, and other
gross metals, may become gold ;—a bitter fruit,
sweet : that a crystal, capable of breaking,
may acquire the hardness of adamant ; a leper,
a gouty person, or a paralytic, may recover
their original vigour.   Thus, their want of
judgment makes them accuse sages of impos-
ture, and philosophers of error, because they
have openly averred that this universal remedy,
this Catholic balm, and elixir of life, was not
only possible, but that they themselves had
made and acknowledged by experience, all the
results which they attributed to it.

" This deplorable ignorance has, in our day,
become so strongly rooted, that the greatest
lights are not too dazzling to dissipate it. And
as it is long ago since it had its origin in the
world, its darkness is the more intense. It has
swollen as a rivulet, that widens as it removes
farther from its source; and I may say, that it

has reached such a point, that the design of enlightening the minds of this our age, might pass for a kind of temerity and presumption.

" Nevertheless, the truth and reality of the philosopher's elixir appears to me so evident, that I would rather expose myself to the censure of ignorant people, than be silent. If I draw down upon me, by this attempt, a host of senseless persecutors, I hope to engage the learned in my defence; and perhaps those who fly into a passion with me, in the face of this apology, will surrender themselves one day to the force of its reasonings. And if, in the commencement of this discourse, they regard me as an excommunicated person, in the end they will treat me as a friend to philosophy. Thus I shall have had the honour to open the door to a work so rich and so advantageous as this is. And that too, in such a manner, that they who, plunged in error, have laboured to the present time guided by a blind desire; and, without a reasonable foundation, built on false and foreign matters to the prejudice of their time, their pains, and their property, will happily know the truth, and the source from whence they must extract it. At least I shall enjoy the pleasure of having laboured for the public good, combated contempt, and advocated the side of truth. These are the principal reasons which engage me in this undertaking; and which oblige me to shew the world, to the great scorn of the ignorant, that the Elixir of the Philosophers is a work possible in nature, provided that it be aided and assisted by art; and this shall be the result of the following reasonings."

With what delightful simplicity this good man writes; and with what energy he denounces the ignorance of the times! How proudly does he submit to the ridicule he anticipates; and with what self-complacency does he look forward to the period in which his arguments will have converted an infidel world! And then his disinterested views "for the public good!" Nothing can be better. He must have been among the latest votaries (and perhaps *victims*) of Alchymy. The eighteenth century was at hand: and yet a churchman could sit down and seriously undertake to prove the existence of the Philosopher's Stone, —could prescribe rules for its discovery, and conceive it little short of blasphemy to deny it the most ample credence! This tone and style of writing, besides conveying fully and fairly the exploded tenets of Alchymy, gives an uncommon value to the book; and I have it in contemplation to array it in an English garb, and present it to that portion of the public who feel an interest in tracing the progress of the human mind, and in musing upon the aberrations of human reason!

Saturday, 30th April.——Passed Ostia, situated near the mouth of the Tiber, and celebrated for the scene of ancient merry-making. Rome was not visible, from the prevalence of mist: but it is not more than sixteen or eighteen miles from Ostia.

Sunday, THE FIRST OF MAY.——

> " Worship, O ye that lovers bene, this *May!*
>   For of your bliss the calends are begun;
>   And sing with us, away, winter away!
>   Come summer, come, the sweet season and sun;
>   Awake for shame, that have your heavens won;
>   And amorously lift up your headés all——
>   Thank love, that lists you to his merry call."

Thus sings a royal poet, King James I. of Scotland*, in a style and with a feeling for

* See " *The Quair,*" Canto ii. st. 15.

which few crowned heads have been celebrated
—few even of those among whom poetry seems
more congenial, the " Squires of Low Degree."
King James's poetry is little known; less known
than it ought to be. His sorrows and his songs
are almost wholly forgotten; and they would
have been entirely so, perhaps, but for Irving's
paper in " the Sketch Book."

The month of MAY is redolent of many
pleasing recollections. It brings back again
the days of childhood, with all its joyous feelings; the escape from the nursery, and the
exuberance of animal delight, with which we
bounded over the green turf, " dewy with
nature's tear-drops." We weave the wreath
of May-flowers afresh, and triumphantly decorate ourselves with a rustic coronet. Again,
in imagination, " we walk into the sweet mea-
dows and green woods, there to rejoice our
spirits with the beauty and savour of sweet
flowers, and with the noise of birds, praising
God in their kind *." And yet what days
may have intervened since that period and the

* Stowe, speaking of the ancient usages of a May-day
morning.

present,—what months of vanity, and wearisome nights ! Alas ! the recollection, gratifying as it is, seems but like wild flowers springing above a grave ; associated, at the same moment, with thistles and hemlock !

Monday, 2d May.—We were nearly becalmed this evening off the Island of Elba. The moon rose transcendantly beautiful, and poured down a silver rivulet of light upon the quiet surface of the ocean. The rocky coast of Elba lay upon our left in the shade of its own loftiness ; and the air was so temperate, the ship, with her sky-sails set, looked so stately, the waters were so deeply blue and still, the moon so bright and pure, that it had *almost* the feeling of enchantment.

Tuesday, 3d May.—It is impossible to converse long with Lord Hastings and not derive some valuable information. His remarks relative to India, are very entertaining, and interest me exceedingly. To-day the *unicorn* coming upon the *tapis,* his lordship observed, that he had no doubt of its actual existence. During his presidency in India, a native from the interior was desired to sketch out such animals as he had seen, with charcoal ; and to

give some description of their mode of life, for
the purpose of ascertaining whether he was
familiar with any that were unknown to Europeans.   Amongst the rest, he drew a unicorn,
at the same time being totally ignorant of the
curiosity attached to it. It was delineated with
the horn somewhat curved, and (I think his
lordship said) fluted.   Its feet resembled those
of a stag, and its tail was curled or twisted like
that of a pig. The communication thus made,
was immediately acted upon.   Lord Hastings
sent the drawing to one of the native princes,
an ally of the British, and one who had received considerable favours at their hands,
with a request that he would signify whether
such a thing existed, and whether it were possible to obtain a specimen.   The answer was
satisfactory. It stated, that though the animal
had occasionally been taken, yet that it was by
no means common; that it was extremely fleet
of foot, ferocious, and shy ; that they were only
enabled to obtain them by penetrating to their
haunts, entirely covered with green branches,
and shooting them from the ambush. He promised withal, to send the first specimen that
could be taken to the governor. It is to be

regretted, that this never came; but the fact of their existence cannot now be discredited. That point may fairly be set at rest.

As I have mentioned the subject of the unicorn, perhaps it will not be disagreeable to many, if I lay before them the ideas of the ancients on this topic. Rejecting what is clearly fabulous, the remainder is not so utterly out of resemblance as to make the description impertinent.

" Monoceros is a beast with one horn, called therefore by the name of *unicorn*; and albeit there be many horned beasts which may improperly be called unicorns, yet that which is the right unicorn indeed, is like unto a colt of two years and a half old, which hath naturally but one horn, and that a very rich one, which groweth out of the middle of his forehead; being a horn of such virtue as is in no beasts' horn besides; which, whilst some have gone about to deny, they have secretly blinded the eyes of the world from their full view of the greatness of God's great works. For were it not said that the horn were excellent and of surpassing power, I persuade myself it would never be doubted whether there were an uni-

corn or no. But that there is such a peculiar
beast, the Scripture, both in Deuteronomy,
Isaiah, Job, and the Book of Psalms, doth bear
us witness. In all which places how do ex-
positors translate the original word, but thus,
unicorns, or *monoceros*, which, in English, is
an unicorn?

"And again, it is the testimony of Ludovi-
cus Vertomannus, alleged by Gesner, Topsell,
and others, that he himself saw a couple of
the true unicorns at Mecca, in Arabia; one
whereof had a horn of three cubits, being of
the bigness of a colt two years and a half old.
The other was much less, and his horn shorter,
about a span long, for it was but young; and
both these were sent to the sultan of Mecca,
for a rare present, by the king of Ethiopia, who
ever desireth to be in league with the said
sultan, thinking nothing too dear to maintain
his amity. And certainly he could not send
him a gift more welcome, especially this being
a beast so rare, and seldom seen; which may
be, in regard that it is a creature delighting in
nothing more than in a remote and solitary life.

"The colour of these thus sent, was like a
weasel-coloured horse, the head like the head

of a hart, the neck not very long, and the mane growing all on one side; their legs slender and lean, like the legs of an hind; the hoofs on the fore-feet cloven, and the hinder legs somewhat shaggy. The nearest (of any beast better known) is the Indian ass, and Indian horse; excepting that their hoofs are whole, and not cloven, and their colour somewhat differing. For there is a horn grows out between their two eyes like to the true unicorn. By which it appeareth, that of unicorns there is one principal kind only; the rest are less principal, and subordinate to him whose horn is the strongest, sharpest, and of the greatest virtue. For in granting more kinds than one, I do not understand every beast with one horn; but only such *monocerots* as have in their horns virtue against poison,—like unto those horses of India mentioned but even now; and of which Mr. Topsell writeth, that they have harts' heads, and one horn, of which their kings and princes make cups to drink their drink against poison, finding a great preservative to be in the said horn. Munster saith, that the king of Ethiopia hath some store of these beasts; and Mr. Topsell nameth two kingdoms in India (the one talled *Niem,* the other *Lamber,*) which be likewise stored with them.

"Moreover, concerning the horn, it is neither light nor hollow, nor yet smooth like other horns ;—but hard as iron, rough as any file, revolved into many plates, sharper than any dart, straight and not crooked, and everywhere black, except at the top or point. It hath many sovereign virtues, and with an admirable dexterity expelleth poison : insomuch, that being put upon a table furnished with many junkets and banquetting dishes, it will quickly descry whether there be any poison or venom amongst them.—For if there be, then presently the horn is covered with a kind of sweat or dew. And (as it is reported) when this beast cometh to drink, he first dippeth his horn in the water, that thereby he may drive away the poison when venomous beasts have drunk before him.

"And again, I find it recorded, that the Indian and Ethiopian hunters catch of those unicorns which be in their country, after this manner.—They take a goodly, strong, and beautiful young man, whom they cloath in the apparel of a woman, besetting him with divers flowers and odoriferous spices, setting him where the unicorns use to come; and when they see this young man, whom they take to be a woman, they come very lovingly and lay their heads down in his lap, (for above all creatures, they do great reverence to virgins and young maids,) and then the hunters, having notice given them, suddenly come, and finding him asleep, they will deal so with him as that, before he goeth, he must leave his horn behind him.*."

Part of the above may be seen in Pliny; with reference to whom, Lord Hastings well observed, that most of the marvels mentioned in his Natural History, might, in all probability, be found to have some origin in fact: and he supplied a very singular illustration. Pliny notices a people of India (and he is followed by the notorious Sir John Mandeville) who possessed but one leg, placed centrically, and whom he speaks of as rapid runners. This fable may have had foundation in a people called *Bundēlas,* who are accustomed, when they

* Swan's " Speculum Mundi, or a Glasse representing the face of the world." P. 435, et seq. 1635.

enter into the presence of a superior, *to stand on one leg* so long as they remain there. This peculiarity Lord Hastings frequently observed; and no entreaties could prevail on them to dispense a moment with the custom while they conversed with him. The whole circumstance is strongly analogous to the fable of the centaurs; who, being greater equestrians than their neighbours, were said to be half man and half horse.

Thursday, 5th May.—Still calm, and our course scarcely perceptible. Last evening the sun disappeared behind the island of Corsica, and exhibited the most diversified and gorgeous colours that I ever witnessed. An immense Grampus was sporting about the ship, and breathed so sonorously as almost to supply us with a gale.

Friday, 6th May.—Anchored off Villa Franca this morning—a small fortified town about a mile distant from Nice. It is beautifully situated at the bottom of a winding bay. The place itself is villainous; but the bold rocky shore, covered with olive-trees and villas, gives considerable interest to the picture. On first communicating with the commandant of

the fortress of Villa Franca, we were astounded
to hear that five-and-twenty days, including
the voyage, was the regular quarantine. But
this evening better news has reached us, and
we expect pratique on the morrow.

Monday, 9th May.——After considerable va-
riation in the reports relative to pratique, a
few of the officers of the ship with the family
of the Marquis of Hastings were permitted to
land at two o'clock this day. An invitation to
dine with the Governor of Nice having been
previously received, Lieut. Christie, Lieut.
Smart, and myself, accompanied Captain Hamilton on shore. It was the intention of the
latter to sail the same evening, but the wind
being unfavourable, orders were issued to have
all in readiness for weighing by day-light the
ensuing morning. We saw very little of Nice,
but the approach to it is exceedingly fine. In
the foreground are olive groves, to the left a
precipitous rock crowned by a citadel. Monte
Calvo, so called from its barren aspect, rears
itself proudly in the distance, forming part of
the chain of the Maritime Alps. About three
miles from Nice commences the French fron-
tier, separated from Piedmont by the little

river Var, (now dried-up) beyond which boundary, saith a sagacious French tourist *, the fire-fly, so abundant in the country around Nice, never adventures. The cause of this rigid abstinence from a trespass to which the "denizens of air," (as, I think, Darwin affectedly calls them,) have a peculiar claim, is not very obvious; nor, as it appears to me, is the fact very clearly substantiated.

The governor dined at three o'clock. We were ushered into an apartment which was darkened to exclude the sun. The dining-room, darker still, was illuminated by a crowd of wax candles; and thus, if we did not "burn day-light," we burnt the day. The room was small; and the party rather large, at least, large enough to fill it: so that, methinks, the exchange of natural for artificial heat was not altogether judicious. However, the repast was worthy of Gallic science: would that I could say so much for Sardinian taste! For our host marshalled the ladies in one long line, and the gentlemen in another, as if the fair sex had been nothing more than beautiful

* Monsieur Melun.

images; something to look at only, and not
listen to!—I abominate such heathenish inven-
tions!—All that passed worthy of being recorded in this place was an unsuccessful attempt of my own to obtain a *rose!*—Perhaps it
is just as well that it chanced so; that rose might
have been prolific in *thorns!* What a fine
moral! Rochefoucauld is right—" Quelque
difference qui paroisse entre les fortunes, il y a
une certaine compensation de biens et de maux
qui les rend égales."

As the evening advanced we bade farewell
to the family of Lord Hastings, with a regret,
I believe, seldom experienced under circumstances of this nature. But their whole conduct while on board had been so kind and
conciliating—the expression of their good-will
at parting evinced so much amiableness and
excellence of heart, that there was not an
officer of the ship who did not unite in extolling
and in following them with all the best wishes.
Such, indeed, ever result from the exhibition
of good taste and good feeling!

Mr. Tennant also, who had hitherto accompanied us in our wanderings, remained at

Nice, leaving us to indulge the hope that he would rejoin the ship before she left her station. The other passengers forsook us at the same time—" white spirits and black, red spirits and grey,"—for we have had them of all colours !

Tuesday, 10*th May*.—Sailed for Malta at an early hour this morning, with a light wind, which has continued pretty nearly all the day.

Saturday, 14*th May*.—The wind called a *Tramontano* has for several days past carried us at the rate of six or seven knots an hour : the weather is delightfully mild.

Tuesday, 17*th May*.—Arrived very early in the morning at Malta, after beating about all night off the island. It blew hard, and was too dark for us to enter the preceding evening.

It is with no small satisfaction that by the arrival of his majesty's ship Rose (Hon. Captain Abbot,) we learn the promotion of my friend Marsham to the rank of commander, arising solely from the capture of the Greek pirates, recorded in a foregoing chapter. Although we shall lose him by the circumstance, yet it is of a nature too important and too reputa-

ble to permit regret to overpower the plea-
surable feelings which should and which do
attend his preferment.   Long may he live to
enjoy it !

The senior midshipman, Mr. Smaile, was at
the same time, and for the same cause, pro-
moted to the rank of lieutenant.   We are conveying the Greek pirates to Hydra to be delivered up to the government.

Thursday, 19*th May*.——Left Malta with a
fine wind for the Archipelago.   Captain Marsham came out with us a couple of miles, and
on quitting the ship was warmly cheered by
the crew.   A better dispositioned man does not
exist upon the face of the earth, nor one with
a heart more open to every generous and honourable feeling.   During the time that we have
been together, placed too as we necessarily have
been in hourly intercourse, sufficient opportunity has been afforded for the discovery of even
the minutest turn of character.   Nor have I
neglected in this instance what is my constant
practice in others ; and I think it a duty, no
less than it is a pleasure and a pride to me, to
enter in this page of my Journal my impartial

testimony to his merits. If people deserve censure when they do amiss, they are equally entitled to praise when they do well. And mine, however trivial and unimportant it may be accounted, shall not be withheld when I see a cause, and *such* cause, to record it!

The elder son of Sir Manley Power accompanies us on this voyage; and there is Anarguros Condouriotti, a nephew of the Greek chief, on board, with a Greek damsel, to whom Captain Hamilton gives a passage.

Saturday Morning, 21st May.—Between the Island of Cerigo and the South coast of the Morea. We have sailed at the rate of ten knots in the hour nearly all the way from Malta. Our present destiny is Milo, and then, probably, Alexandria: since the news of the death of the Pacha of Egypt reached us on the morning previous to our departure from Malta, the captain is extremely anxious about it: but circumstances may change our plans, and the rumour is not well authenticated.

Whit-Sunday, 22d May.—Off Milo, but not likely to touch at present. The report here is, that ten days ago six Greek fire-ships, having been sent into the Bay of Modon, where the Turkish fleet then lay, *twenty-seven* of them were consumed, of which four were frigates, and eight corvettes. This is great news, if true: but alas! "c'est trop bon, pour être vrai."

Monday, 23d May.—Arrived off Hydra. It is delightful to find that the news relative to the destruction of the Turkish fleet (with which were four *Austrian merchantmen* that had been used as transports) is quite correct. Besides this, Modon, a Turkish possession, has been reduced and burnt. A boat came along side of us just now containing several Greeks; amongst them is a nephew of the Admiral Miaoulis, and Tombasis, a member of the senate, and brother of him who formerly commanded the Greek fleet. They are both fine looking men, but the countenance of the latter is extremely prepossessing. There was likewise a Mr. Masson, (a Scotch gentleman) who has been residing at Hydra several months, and who speaks enthusiastically of the amiable and intellectual qualities of the principal people.

11

Colocotroni is still here, but has almost made his peace, and is laying down plans for the ensuing campaign. Mr. Masson thinks he is not so bad as report represents him. This may be, or not; but the Greeks should be careful of entrusting him again with too much power;— he is certainly a dangerous man. Ambition and avarice cannot co-exist with patriotism— scarcely with probity.

Mr. Masson, it appears, has fixed himself at Hydra for the purpose of establishing a *college* there, and of presiding over the establishment. He instructs several young Greeks in English, and seems to be greatly respected by the primates, who listen to him (he says) with much deference. This accounts for his admiration and praise : but still, as I understand that he does not possess any further means of assisting them than by his own individual efforts, the fact speaks favourably for both parties. They are endeavouring to scrape together a library.

I lost an opportunity of landing at Hydra this morning, and we sail for Napoli di Romania to-morrow. But our return in a few days is pretty certain; and we shall be here frequently: so that many occasions of investigating this place and people are likely to arise. There are two Englishmen at present there, beside the Scotchman above mentioned; their names I forget.

Our old friends the "*pirates*," departed with Tombasis. They are to be placed on board a Greek vessel of war; and will thus have the means of effacing the dishonourable stain attached to their late proceedings. Amongst other circumstances of moment, we have learnt to-day, that the Greeks expect, in less than a couple of months, two large frigates, built in America, and equipped with every requisite. These vessels have been provided at the expence of certain Englishmen; and it must be confessed, that the measures they are *now* adopting, are much more likely to be of service than any, or than all their previous undertakings. Vessels of magnitude, sufficient to cope with the larger ships of the enemy, and to enable them to strike a sure and effective blow;——to take advantage of opportunity, and, by some resolute and well-concerted plan, to seize and employ the finely-modelled ships of the line, which the Turks so uselessly construct, are objects of the deepest and most vital importance. And all this may be effected by the frigates about to be delivered to them. Men and officers are already prepared; and they only wait their arrival to begin with loftier pretensions, and more assured success.

END OF VOL. I.

Printed by R. GILBERT, St. John's Square, London.

Check Out More Titles From HardPress Classics Series In this collection we are offering thousands of classic and hard to find books. This series spans a vast array of subjects – so you are bound to find something of interest to enjoy reading and learning about.

Subjects:
Architecture
Art
Biography & Autobiography
Body, Mind &Spirit
Children & Young Adult
Dramas
Education
Fiction
History
Language Arts & Disciplines
Law
Literary Collections
Music
Poetry
Psychology
Science
…and many more.

Visit us at www.hardpress.net

CPSIA information can be obtained
at www.ICGtesting.com
Printed in the USA
BVHW081812190819
556220BV00016B/1448/P